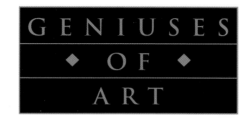

GENIUSES
◆ OF ◆
ART

NATIONAL MUSEUM OF ANTHROPOLOGY, MEXICO

◆

GENIUSES
◆ OF ◆
ART

NATIONAL MUSEUM OF ANTHROPOLOGY, MEXICO

◆

susaeta

Scientific Co-ordination:
Juan-Ramón Triadó Tur
Titular Professor of History of Art,
University of Barcelona

Text:
Laura García Sánchez
Doctor in History of Art

Translated by:
Carole Patton

Illustrations:
CONACULTA. –INAH. – MEX

Reproductions authorised by the:
Instituto Nacional de Antropología e Historia

The Editors wish to express their gratitude to the
Museum Authorities
for making this book possible

Cover Design:
Paniagua & Calleja

CONTENTS

Funerary Mask
Classic Period (A.D. 1-650);
volcanic stone, turquoise, coral,
shell and obsidian;
height: 21.7 cm; width: 20 cm

As a sample of the archaeological treasures
housed in the Museum, masks, which
concealed the divinity of the gods, were
used by priests in the great religious
ceremonies of the Teotihuacan culture. The
stylised eyebrows, the flower in the middle
of the forehead and the stepped-fret
decoration on the nose give it a more
distinguished aspect.

Reproduction of the Inside of a House

The ethnography presented at the Museum
is a fundamental part of Mexican reality,
being its roots and, at the same time, its
trunk and its fruits. By means of objects
and written ideas, the intention is to show
the homogeneities and differences of the
country's indigenous cultures, as well as the
ways of conduct that give meaning to their
life.

A Living Monument to the Indigenous Cultures of Mexico

The richness of the archaeological and ethnographical collections housed in Mexico's National Museum of Anthropology makes it one of the most important institutions of its kind in the world. Besides the architectural beauty of the building itself, the valuable exhibits housed herein together with a coherent museographical project have turned it into the best introduction to the study of the country's cultural roots, thus handing down a great and glorious past to the people of Mexico.

One of the main objectives of the museum is that of displaying the magnificence of the pre-Hispanic cultures that inhabited the lands which today are Mexico, the changes they underwent on encountering the Europeans, and the current situation of the native peoples of this territory. A trip through the various exhibition galleries rewards the visitor with a living lesson of Art and History, where one is able to experience the indigenous world during its different periods, and breathe in the magical atmosphere of Antiquity.

Its treasures have gradually increased over the years by means of ongoing donations, archaeological findings and acquisitions. However, like any other great museum, its process of gestation and consolidation is deeply rooted in time and space.

A Few Historical Notes on the Museum

Since the second half of the 18th century, as a result of what we could call a growing feeling of nationalism, the Mexican people began to take interest in their native heritage and ethnography. The awareness of being the inheritor of two civilisations, the Mesoamerican and the Spanish, made them consider their culture from a new perspective, now enriched by a markedly different spirit and which had to be known and valued precisely for representing the union of two pasts that gave the country its own personality. Consequently, the fact that the first archaeological research on monuments, sometimes patronised by the Spanish monarchy, corresponds to that period or that the monoliths discovered by chance in Mexico City were studied and preserved should come as no surprise to us.

The first collection to form part of the current museum dates from the end of the eighteenth century. Shortly before 1775, Viceroy Bucareli ordered all the previously abandoned ancient Mexican documents to be taken to the Royal Pontifical University of Mexico. Great part of them were in fact those gathered years before by Lorenzo Boturini, an Italian who had come to the city to administer the estate belonging to the descendants of Hernán Cortés who held an important collection of pictographic codices. This decision led to the first compilation that could be of some use to researchers.

Some years later, to be exact, on 13th August 1790, the statue of Coatlicue, the Mexica Mother Goddess, was found when work was being carried out on the *Plaza Mayor* of Mexico City, and on 17th December of that same year workers unearthed the Sun Stone, belonging to the same culture as the first statue and popularly known as the Aztec Calendar.

For the first time, instead of being destroyed, these imposing stones were preserved by order of Viceroy Revillagigedo, who sent the statue of Coatlicue to the newly-established University Museum, the first institution of its kind in the country, whilst the Sun Stone was placed at the foot of one of the cathedral walls. A further four such monuments were found on the same site between 1791 and 1792, which, together with minor objects, made up the nucleus of a future, more dignified museum, promoting the first investigations based on ancient findings carried out in the national territory and arousing at the same time a national consciousness that the cultural heritage of Mexico had to be preserved.

Some time later, toward the end of the colonial period, to be precise, in June 1808, Viceroy Iturrigaray formed an Antiquity Board, the first antecedent of today's National Institute of Anthropology and History, in order to give the archaeological artefacts of the past a certain official character.

The end of the War of Independence brought with it a resurgence of indigenous nationalism which led the Mexicans to being more interested in their native culture. These reasons, together with the fact that the archaeological findings that were continually taking place in the Valley and City of Mexico ended up being stored up on university premises, led two presidents, Guadalupe Victoria and Anastasio Bustamante, to passing a decree to found the National Museum, which was formally carried out on 18th March 1825, but its head office was still at the University.

Like so many other cultural facilities of the period, from that moment on, all kinds of objects belonging to natural history and the pre-Hispanic indigenous world, as well as historical documents, were gathered together here, providing testimony of Mexico's recent past. The different museums existing today, each of which specialises in different areas of research, all have their origin in this museum.

However, it must be said that in those days the true meaning of the museum was not fully understood, nor was it of nationwide importance. It is clear that, in accordance with the fashion of the period, it was used to house, in a somewhat disorderly manner, a number of objects which increased over the years.

The Museum's First Independent Location

For over forty years there were several unsuccessful attempts to house the museum in its own facilities. Eventually, in July 1866, thanks to the initiative of Emperor Maximilian of Hapsburg, who, from a political point of view and for reasons of space, destined the old building of the Royal Mint, where precious metals were smelted and coins struck, for this purpose.

The building was a beautiful palace dating from the days of Felipe II, standing on the *Calle de la Moneda* and in the extensive area of buildings adjacent to the National Palace, in the historical quarter of Mexico City. This new location

The Goddess Coatlicue
Post-Classic Period (A.D. 900-1521),
volcanic stone,
height: 350 cm; width: 130 cm

This great sculpture from the Mexica region represents the Mother Goddess Coatlicue, discovered in 1790 in the main square of Mexico City. The upper part consists of two serpent heads facing one another, the symbol of duality and an animal that is connected with the Underworld, whilst on the lower part we can observe eagle talons instead of feet.

9

Photographs

Some of the best pieces of the then emergent museum (left, ca. 1885) were initially displayed in the patio of the former Royal Mint, whilst the Monolith Gallery (above, ca. 1895) in time became one of the first galleries to have a certain scientific rigorousness. President Porfirio Díaz (below, ca. 1905), solemnly poses in front of the new emplacement of the Sun Stone.

gave the museum its well-earned setting. The huge monoliths were moved there and later placed in the patio, whilst the collections of archaeology, geology, zoology, etc. as well as the furniture and documents belonging to the colonial period and to that of the War of Independence were arranged, in accordance with the knowledge of the period, in the galleries. This was until 1964 when the museum moved into its current building.

As time went by, the old museum became a fertile environment for the study of the ancient pre-Hispanic cultures of Mexico and, in general, of the country's history. Some of the most important specialists of the times were formed here and it was where the structural changes that would affect its fields of research were engendered. In 1877 the institution was divided into three departments: Natural History, Anthropology and History, continuing its development as a centre of education and scientific controversy. A decade later, in 1887, the sections of Anthropology and Ethnography were created, and President Porfirio Díaz inaugurated the Monolith Gallery where all the large pre-Hispanic sculptures discovered until then were put on display. In the largest gallery of the museum, where silver and gold had been formerly smelted, the sculptural monuments, silent witnesses of the diverse native cultures of the country, were placed without fol-

Sun Stone or Aztec Calendar
Post-Classic Period (A.D. 900-1521), basalt, diameter: 358 cm

Carved during the reign of Axayácatl (1469-1481), this huge sculpture commemorates the era of the Fifth Sun. The latter is represented in the centre by the face of Tonatiuh, surrounded by the four previous suns. It is also known as the Aztec Calendar because of the numerous signs related to the subject.

lowing any specific order or chronological criteria. The imposing Sun Stone, since then the symbol of pre-Hispanic indigenous Mexico, stood out in the middle of the gallery.

During the early years of the twentieth century, thanks to the level of scientific progress and development that archaeology and anthropology had attained by then, the correct chronological order of the different primitive cultures could be properly worked out. Parallel to this, in 1909 the decision was taken to separate the natural history section in order to create a Natural History Museum, the museum at this point being known as the National Museum of Archaeology, History and Ethnography. And so it was called until 1939 when, by express wish of President Lázaro Cárdenas, the National Institute of Anthropology and History was established, and the history collections became part of the corresponding museum, housed in Chapultepec Castle. Since then it is under this institute and is called the National Museum of Anthropology, the contemporary academic definition thus helping to correctly display the finest cultural and artistic testimonies of the peoples of Mexico, as well as to exhibit the main part of its archaeological and ethnographical collections in a coherent and dignified manner.

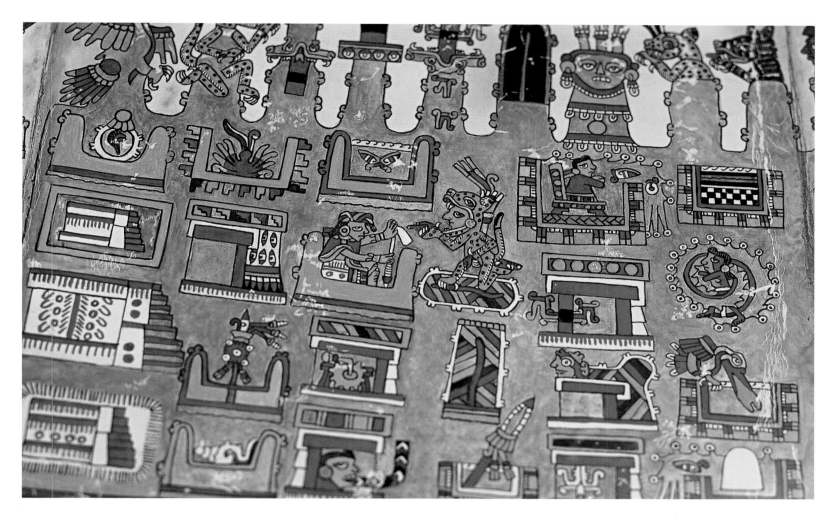

The outcome of the 1910 Mexican Revolution turned out to be in keeping with this technical and scientific determination, the people becoming more conscious, if one might say so, of not having to scorn their double cultural legacy and of the absolute need to not degrade one in favour of the other. And so this is how the old desire to show the ancient civilisation and its evolution to this day finally found its definitive place, thus allowing it to be understood and valued as part of the national spirit, and so contribute to dignifying the native inhabitants of the territory and their culture. The grandeur of the museum building and the beauty of its surroundings and collections also helped to achieve this objective, attracting visitors from all over the country and from abroad.

The Building,
the Pride of the Mexican People

On 17th September 1964 the spectacular new museum located in Chapultepec Forest was inaugurated by the then president of the Republic, Adolfo López Mateos, who unveiled a plaque which read: "The Mexican People erect this monument in honour of the admirable cultures that flourished during the pre-Colombian era in regions which today are part of the Republic. Standing before the testimonies of those cultures, the Mexico of today pays a tribute to indigenous

Main Façade of the National Museum of Anthropology

Featuring the Mexican coat of arms in the centre, the façade was constructed in white marble from Santo Tomás, Puebla, in memory of the considerable use made by the pre-Hispanic cultures of stone as a building material and for artistic works. The building covers an area of 70,000 m², 45,000 being the actual building itself.

Cacaxtla, Fragment of the South Wall
Late Classic Period (ca. A.D. 800),
fresco painting

Famous for its rich painting, on display in the gallery on the Toltec culture, the south wall of the archaeological site of Cacaxtla features a person standing on a feathered serpent and flanked by aquatic animals. His body painted black, his large bird headdress and other attributes relate him maybe to Quetzalcóatl.

Mexico, acknowledging characteristics of its national singularity". Apart from being in a place that is easily accessible for national and foreign visitors, the museum is located in what is considered to be one of the loveliest and most favourite natural beauty spots of Mexico City.

After two years of plans and calculations, it was finally built over a period of only 19 months, being in charge of the project and its coordination the architect Pedro Ramírez Vázquez. In turn, he was assisted by the architects Rafael Mijares and Jorge Campuzano, together with a team of 42 engineers and 52 architects, who supervised the works being carried out by a numerous "army" of workmen and artisans.

As to the specific requirements of the project, some of the most important to bear in mind were the scientific and educational purposes of the museum as well as the divulgation of its contents. In this way, instead of merely gathering, exhibiting and preserving the treasures belonging to ancient and modern cultures, the educational objective was of prime importance, as well as an overall view of the human being.

An interdisciplinary group of professionals made up of anthropologists, historians, museologists, artists, ethnographers and educationists also took part. Not

View of the Great Central Patio,
From Outside the Mexica Gallery Looking Towards the Foyer

This splendid and imposing patio attracts the visitor to the Museum. In the centre, and surrounded by water, there is a metal conch, symbolising the wind, and which sometimes sounds, thus imitating the way of calling in the indigenous world and reminding us of the emblem of the great god Quetzalcóatl. Its size gives us an idea of the magnificence of the place.

only did Ramírez Vázquez take their recommendations into account, but he also promoted special ethnographical and archaeological explorations, organised the transportation of large archaeological objects from various regions all over the country, supervised the removal of all the contents from the former facilities, ordered the classification and cataloguing of all the funds by means of an electronic system, as well as being in charge of the museum premises, the training of 50 bilingual guides, the issue of commemorative medals and the edition of two memorandums. The future museum also received numerous collections of works from private fields. As a whole, the museum funds were increased by approximately 4,000 objects of great historic and aesthetic value.

All these tasks were carried out at the same time as its construction and the preparation of the different sections. So, with the aid of all the modern technical and museological instruments of the time, the main objective was to present the origin, the evolution and the contributions of the pre-Hispanic cultures, as well as the life and culture peculiar to the indigenous groups of Mexico.

The architectonic solution did not forget the specific requirements of its functioning as an institution and that of housing and appropriately exhibiting its cultural legacies in a contemporary way not too inconsistent with their origin. A considerable part of this great building was inspired by pre-Hispanic architecture, though modern technologies and materials were also used as they were related to the requirements and conditions of the environment and of man with his own epoch. This conscious desire of Mexican architecture to be in keeping with its origin can be observed in the solid dignity and adornment of the museum, where the influence of the Governor's House of the Uxmal archaeological site may be detected, and, more specifically, on the second floor of the building, whose serpent-like latticework reminds us of ancient Mayan decoration. Consequently, it was demonstrated that architecture before the arrival of the Spanish, that of the colonial period, and modern architecture express, in spite of their different techniques and formal solutions, the influence of the geographical environment, the generous use of space, the conservation of the natural textures and colours of the materials or plastic continuity perpetuated through the artisan.

Since the main purpose of the museum was an educational one, it was necessary to take many psychological factors regarding the conception of interior and exterior spaces into account. In line with this philosophy, a frame had to be provided for a peaceful atmosphere in which the visitor could quietly gaze at or contemplate the exhibits, even at the busiest of times. The need for a space that would allow a great number of people to freely circulate and visit the different galleries either by following an itinerary or in the order chosen by the visitor, as well as the challenge of finding a way so that the public could make the most of their time at the museum, meant that the galleries had to be grouped around a central area. This was also a classical characteristic of Mayan architecture, known as a "quadrangle", consisting of a kind of patio surrounded by buildings, but communicating with the outside by means of openings on the corners, thus keeping the outside present on the inside.

In this way, and in order to avoid the visitor feeling overwhelmed by such a vast museum, most of the exhibition galleries were designed overlooking the park, and distributed in a way that one cannot visit more than two galleries without having, on the upper floor, a magnificent view over the patio —inspired by the architecture of the Uxmal Nunnery Quadrangle- and, on the lower floor, having to go out into the patio to take a rest.

The four elements of nature, ever-present in the cosmovision of ancient cultures, are represented in the patio: water, earth, wind and fire. An inverted pyramid or umbrella-shaped ceiling covers part of this space, at the same time as it leaves it open. The "umbrella" is also a fountain from which water cascades down from its round centre around an imposing column that is adorned with bronze reliefs. The latter were sculpted by the brothers José and Tomás Chávez Morado, being inspired by the four cardinal points and depict events belonging to the history of Mexico.

Column in the Patio

The umbrella-shaped structure in the central patio is considered a jewel of modern architecture. Supported by metal ties, it rests on a column covered with wrought iron, which is decorated in interesting reliefs, thus contributing to embellish the content of the galleries from the outside.

Wall Painting Depicting *Everyday Scenes*
Jacobo Rodríguez Padilla

"Take care of the things of the earth,
Do something: cut wood, plough the land,
Plant nopals, plant magueys,
You'll have something to drink, something
[to eat, and something to wear;
Thus you will stand, you'll be true,
thus you will walk.
Thus you'll be spoken of, you'll be praised,
thus you will make yourself known."

Huehuetlatolli

Museum Layout and Cultural Activities

The museum was designed so that it could offer a scientifically exact presentation which, at the same time, would be so attractive from an aesthetic point of view that a visit here would be considered a true spectacle. As soon as you enter the foyer on the ground floor, you will find an information panel with a plan of the museum so that visitors may determine their own itinerary for visiting the exhibits. You will immediately go into the Temporary Exhibition Gallery where a bright and harmonic mural in the form of a multicoloured map by Luis Covarrubias, depicting the cultural aspects characterising the vast area known as Mesoamerica, welcomes the visitor.

Immediately after this are the Archaeology Galleries, dedicated to the pre-Hispanic cultures and classified in accordance with three criteria: temporary, cul-

Lower Floor. Archaeology Galleries

1. *Indigenous Cultures of Mexico*
2. *Introduction to Anthropology*
3. *Population of America*
4. *Pre-Classic Central High Plateau*
5. *Teotihuacán*
6. *The Toltecs and their Age*
7. *Mexica*
8. *Cultures of Oaxaca*
9. *Cultures of the Gulf Coast*
10. *The Maya*
11. *Cultures of the West*
12. *Cultures of the North*

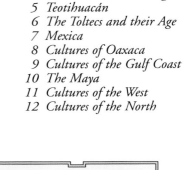

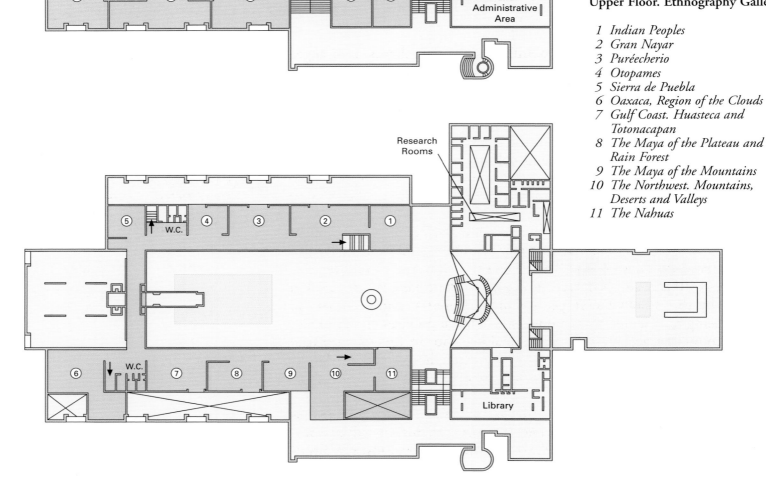

Upper Floor. Ethnography Galleries

1. *Indian Peoples*
2. *Gran Nayar*
3. *Puréecherio*
4. *Otopames*
5. *Sierra de Puebla*
6. *Oaxaca, Region of the Clouds*
7. *Gulf Coast. Huasteca and Totonacapan*
8. *The Maya of the Plateau and Rain Forest*
9. *The Maya of the Mountains*
10. *The Northwest. Mountains, Deserts and Valleys*
11. *The Nahuas*

tural and regional. After the Introduction to Anthropology, the galleries are arranged in chronological order, starting with the Population of America and continuing with those of the Pre-Classic Central High Plateau, Teotihuacán and The Toltecs and their age. All the galleries display the various stages of development of the cultures of the Mexican Central High Plateau before the advent of the Aztecs, whose gallery, called Mexica, is situated in the centre of the museum. Then we have the galleries displaying the artistic and cultural testimonies of the inhabitants of the most peripheral regions of Mesoamerica: Oaxaca, Gulf Coast, Maya, Western and Northern Mexico. In this order, each of them exhibits the richness of its objects representing pre-Columbian indigenous art.

On the upper floor is the area dedicated to Ethnography, i.e. living indigenous cultures: Indian Peoples, Gran Nayar, Purépecha, Otopames, Sierra de Puebla, Oaxaca, Gulf Coast, the Maya of the Plateau and the Rain Forest, the Maya of the Mountains, Northeast and Nahuas. On display in these galleries we can find artefacts made by the various native peoples of the country, a great variety of ethnic groups being represented from a linguistic-cultural point of view, but also taking into account the geographical areas inhabited. So, in order to reaffirm and transmit that feeling of unity and continuity throughout time, the layout of the Ethnography Galleries tries to correspond with the order of the Archaeology ones.

Since it was designed as a cultural, scientific and amusing institution, the museum was endowed with everything required to guarantee this objective: workshops, laboratories with room for research, storage areas, cellars, three auditori-

Wall Painting Depicting the Map of Mexico
Luis Covarrubias

One grasps a better understanding of the ecological differences of the territory thanks to the definition of the topographical relief and the main geographical changes. In his work, Covarrubias used the most important archaeological discoveries of the different pre-Hispanic cultures represented in the precincts to situate them within a very complex geography.

Tláloc, God of the Rain
*Late Pre-Classic Period
(400 B.C.- A.D. 200), volcanic stone;
height: 8 m; weight 168 t*

*Tláloc, the god of the rain, "he who lies on
the grass", came from Teotihuacán and was
assisted by the Tlaloques, or lesser gods, in
the delightful job of watering the earth.
When summoned, his acolytes would
noisily smash their pitchers causing
thunder, lightning and the welcome rain,
the pillar of life. His partner is
Chalchiuhtlicue, the goddess of the ocean
and running water, who is in fact
represented here, although the sculpture is
named as Tláloc.*

ums, the Eusebio Dávalos Hurtado National Library of Anthropology and History, educational services, annexes, shop, cafeteria, restaurant, etc.

For many years now the institution has updated its technology in accordance with the advances made in the fields of anthropology, history and archaeology, incorporating the latest discoveries and didactic elements applied to an ever-increasing number of exhibits. If we add to this the reforms carried out on the building and gardens, the digitisation of inventories and catalogues, the reorganisation of the educational services, facilities for the disabled, and the galleries, there is no doubt that we are talking about one of the best equipped and most efficient museums in the world as well as one of the most renowned cultural centres.

Nevertheless, we cannot forget the interest shown by well-known contemporary artists in emphasising the beauty of the premises inside through their contribution of important works of art in the way of murals, oil paintings, stained glass, acrylics, latticework, tapestries, etc. Some of these artists are: Raúl Anguiano, Leonora Carrington, José Chávez Morado, Rafael Coronel, Luis Covarrubias, Arturo Estrada, Manuel Felguérez, Arturo García Bustos, Mathias Goeritz, Jorge González Camarena, Iker Larrauri, Carlos Mérida, Adolfo Mexiac, Nicolás Moreno, Pablo O'Higgins, Nadine Prado, Fanny Rabel, Pedro Ramírez Vázquez, Jacobo Rodríguez Padilla, Regina Raúll, Valeta Swan, Rufino Tamayo, Antonio Trejo or Alfredo Zalce. As soon as you arrive at the museum, you encounter the enormous stone monolith known as Tláloc, the rain god of the Teotihuacan culture (4th-6th centuries), found in a riverbed near Coatlinchán, about 45 kilometres from Mexico City. Because of an old superstition, the local inhabitants were concerned that if it were removed and taken elsewhere, then the area would be hit by drought. Luckily, the old village teacher managed to convince them that this would not occur. Therefore, this imposing figure nearly 8 metres in height and 168 tons in weight welcomes visitors to the museum and symbolises the anthropological content of the place.

An Introduction to Anthropology

In order to show us the place occupied by the cultures of ancient and modern Mexico in the world, the first exhibition one finds on entering the National Museum of Anthropology is a modern introduction to the evolutionary process of mankind. By reviewing the great stages of this period, different aspects directly connected with any of the fields of anthropology are presented to us: physical anthropology, archaeology, linguistics and ethnography.

The explanatory analysis of the evolution of the human species is based on change and diversity throughout time, concepts linked by hominization and humanization. The former corresponds with the processes of adaptation and permanence of biological traits that we share with other primates and which in the human being are marked by our bipedism and the development of our brain. Humanization involves all those phenomena which are more strictly human characteristics, such as the making of tools, life in society and, later on, language and abstract ideas.

The first part of the exhibition deals with the evolution of human life on Earth. The origin and evolution of mankind, the place man occupies within the animal kingdom and his relation to other primates are all explained through displays of real fossils or replicas, remains of bones and other findings. In this way, physical anthropology is widely described to the public. It is a discipline that chiefly investigates the links between the biological characteristics of the human being and his cultural activities, whilst one of its branches, paleoanthropology, is becoming more important each day since it is steadily providing us with a deeper knowledge of the origins and evolution of man and his primitive relations.

Osteology allows us to distinguish the structural differences between the male and female skeleton and, through its study, determine the age and any possible anomalies. Anthropologists have been able to identify certain practices such as cranial deformation and teeth mutilation, which are the easiest to recognise. This science points out the characteristics of each of the human groups throughout the world so that we may understand the unity and variety of the human race.

Australopithecus afarensis, "Lucy"
2 million-700,000 B.C.

The technical reconstruction of the hypothetical physical aspect of one of the most important remains for its antiquity and the evidence that upright walking (bipedalism) distinguished this species from the other primates, allows us to appreciate how significant a fossil cranium can be and how important its study is for establishing the beginning of hominization.

Over the millennia, the nomadic tribes crossing the pass which then existed between Asia and America travelled the whole American continent from north to south in search of game. They reached Central America, the Amazon Basin and the Andes, as far as Tierra del Fuego. From this moment onwards, the evolution of the human species had no limits.

Archaeology is the science that deals with the study of human societies of the past by analysing their cultural marks and through material findings. In fact, the work of an archaeologist consists in determining the chronology of remains, putting them together when possible, and interpreting the culture and conduct of the people who made these artefacts. In the corresponding section of this museum, we can observe excavation techniques used by archaeologists and how carefully remains are recovered, besides being explained, through stratigraphy, how it is possible to determine the succession of cultures in time, by deciphering the chronological order of the beginnings of agriculture, pottery, weaving or metallurgy. A comparative chart of the main societies of the past situates the inhabitants of ancient Mexico at the same level as the Egyptians, the primitive dwellers of Mesopotamia and the first ones of India. Various interesting archaeological objects, especially axes, funerary masks, oil containers, sarcophagi, remote inscriptions, etc., are evident signs of the technological evolution of man occurring since prehistoric times until the flourishing of the first civilisations. These artistic manifestations allow the archaeologist to discover ritual ceremonies, everyday customs, technical progresses and also to trace contacts with other cultures.

Next we have the section dedicated to ethnography or the emergence of the genus Homo, destined to explaining what happened between 2 million and 700,000 years B.C. On display here are numerous objects made by different peoples from all over the world, proving that man solves the same problems in similar or various ways, showing how he adapts to life in different ecosystems or environments. Human culture is therefore a constant process of inventiveness and creation, taking advantage of the resources available. Ethnography is closely related to ethnology, a discipline which analyses the differences and similarities existing between cultures and, therefore,

Mural Painting
Detail
José Chávez Morado

The great mural describes the evolution followed by the peoples of ancient Mexico during the development of the "superarea" known as Mesoamerica, from early activities connected with hunting and gathering to the birth of the great cultures. The same as Aridamerica and Oasisamerica, it emerged with the appearance of farming and sedentary peoples around 2500 B.C.

Showcases with Heads and Crania

The various indigenous cultures of Mexico that flourished during pre-Hispanic times, as well as those of today, offer Anthropology a vast field of study and museums valuable exhibit material. Furthermore, they are a good part of the history and cultural legacy of the country, and the knowledge of them grows in importance every day.

Another View of the Introduction to Anthropology Gallery

Methods, techniques and aims make Anthropology a science in which the variety and levels of historical development of its cultures mean that Mexico is a living laboratory. Not only does the gallery dedicated to this discipline justify the name of the museum, but it also serves as a universal framework for the Mexican cultures, situating them correctly in time and space.

between human groups, as well as their historical development and the relations between them.

The penultimate subject corresponds with what has been called the creative revolution, consisting of numerous examples of human cultural production, such as rupestrian painting, the best examples of which are Altamira and Lascaux. The reconstructions of the Shanidar and Dolni Vestonice archaeological sites are proof of a completely human behaviour, since they imply the presence of rituals. All this culminates with the last argument proposed, which represents the current diversity of human beings, showing elements of the history of the life of each individual as well as the history of their relatives and ancestors, their biology, language and culture.

A mural by José Chávez Morado, illustrating the evolution of the peoples and civilisations of the area during the Pre-Classic, Classic and Post-Classic periods, helps to reinforce the intention of the exhibition displayed in this gallery. According to the artist's own definition of his work: "The earth is symbolised by a great female figure where men evolve from nomads to hunters and then to sedentary farmers. Part of the drama of these events is represented by propitiatory dances and other magic rituals. In the centre of the mural, a huge pyramid-man gazes upwards at a starry sky and bears witness to the cultural exploits of the Classic period. The stone structure that emerges from the watery landscape of Tenochtitlán symbolises the Aztec capital; war trade, ceremonies and cultural progresses are shown in the activities of the Post-Classic period immediately before the Conquest".

Archaeology Galleries

Archaeology, defined as the great archives of the past, is a science that has always fascinated man, which is why the galleries dedicated to it play a leading role in this museum, both for the display of the objects belonging to different cultures, as well as for the history engendered in them. The value of an archaeological object depends on its correct interpretation, since the latter provides us with the information regarding the period concerned. As the material is so varied and its chronology so remote, archaeology is now considered as teamwork in which scientists and specialists act together. An archaeologist must have a versatile formation, and the training of new investigators is one of their main responsibilities. Archaeological discoveries are displayed to the public in exhibitions that illustrate the evolution of a culture over different periods.

Population of America. The Origins

Thousands of years before the appearance of the great civilisations of Mesoamerica, the early settlers of the American continent arrived from Asia. They crossed the Bering Strait between the north-east of Asia and Alaska, taking advantage of the retreat of the waters in the area during the last ice age. This was how the first groups began to settle in America, although it is also probable that other routes were followed through the Pacific, especially from Polynesia. This prehistoric age is relatively recent in comparison to the Old World, since it covers a period of approximately 80,000 years.

On entering the gallery dedicated to this era, one sees a mural painting by Iker Larrauri, a magnificent work where we can observe some hunters coming from Asia, following the migrations and the movement of

Fossils Belonging to Fauna of the Pleistocene

The remains of a mammoth discovered in Santa Isabel Ixtapan, near Texcoco, together with some tips of weapons used by hunters to capture these animals when they became trapped on the swampy banks of the lakes, prove the coexistence of man and these great beasts millions of years ago.

Mural Painting
Iker Laurrauri

The settling of man on the American continent is relatively recent: he came to the New World towards the end of the Palaeolithic. Between 70,000 and 100,000 years before our era, tribes of Siberian hunters, who were still nomads, came in successive waves to Alaska during the last period of glaciation.

various groups of large mammals. In the distance, the land of Alaska covered in ice is an invitation to explore unknown lands.

Numerous graphs and maps explain the formation of the glaciers that covered the northern regions of the land, creating a bridge between Asia and America which became known as *Beringia*, and which was the passage for human migrations for a long time. This movement of masses occurred in waves and different groups, over a period of thousands of years, managed to reach the southernmost tip of the American continent, whilst the Inuit —Eskimos-, the last to come into the northern region, have remained there since.

As a complement to the Introduction to Anthropology gallery, part of the area is dedicated to illustrating the oldest period of the hunters and gatherers in

Extinct Fauna of the Pleistocene
Iker Laurrauri

1964, acrylic on canvas,
height: 8 m; width: 9 m

As a visual complement to all the exhibits in the gallery, this mural shows us the main large, swift mammals of the Pleistocene that lived at the same time as prehistoric man and against which the latter fought until they became extinct. He hunted them for reasons of survival, using their bones, skin and meat.

Reconstruction of Sedentary Life

What distinguishes the Old World from the New is the singularity of the progresses made by pre-Columbian peoples in their evolution towards Neolithic techniques, which also explains the gaps existing amongst the native cultures of America and the surprising advances which characterise some of its civilisations.

Mexico. The visitor may therefore get to know the difficult conditions in which these people had to live, on rocky ledges or in caverns, where they would take shelter from the elements. They knew how to make fire and cut hard stone such as silex and obsidian, with which they made a wide range of efficient tools and other artefacts used for various purposes. Another complement is a large mural describing the fauna of the Pleistocene, represented by a great number of animals (mammoths, bison, horses) which were used for food and clothing by the inhabitants of the New World. The discovery of bone remains of those men and women has enabled experts to reconstruct their physical aspect, know their height, illnesses and other characteristics. In addition to this, some of the best-preserved skulls belonging to the ancient dwellers of the Central High Plateau of Mexico are on display here, their age having been worked out thanks to the carbon-14 method.

Another section shows us the different techniques used for cultivating the land, indicating the beginning of the development of Mesoamerica during its first stage, that is, the period of farming societies. When large mammals began to disappear, hunters gradually stopped being nomads and started to become more attached to the land and to gathering wild plants and fruits. This is how they gradually came to a controlled exploitation of nourishing plants, agriculture allowing these human groups sufficient continuity, security and organisation to be able to develop a civilising activity. This meant an important control of their harsh natural environment, besides showing the possibilities of their creative capacity.

Pre-Classic Cultures

Pre-Classic cultures originated in village groups that began to farm in the Central High Plateau, their historical-cultural evolution being divided into three main periods: Early or Lower (2500-1200 B.C.), Middle (1200-400 B.C.) and Late or Upper (400 B.C. –A.D. 1 or 200). The Pre-Classic Period is the first one that can be correctly labelled as Mesoamerican, and was when some of the cultural elements that would characterise societies of later periods appeared and developed.

The Early Pre-Classic Period was marked by the establishment of sedentary populations, a sign that a sufficient degree of development had been reached regarding farming. Agriculture allowed man to settle down in places and control his food supply, as well as develop his craftsmanship and examine the world in which he lived. This led to the building of huts *(jacales)* and the appearance of the first villages –which were scarcely populated-, the cult to the dead, pottery, weaving and other cultural progresses.

During this period, some groups settled in El Arbolillo, Zacatento and Tlatilco, on the shores of the great lake of the Mexico Basin, whilst others did so in several places throughout the valley of Tehuacán.

Their diet was based on maize, pumpkin, beans and chilli

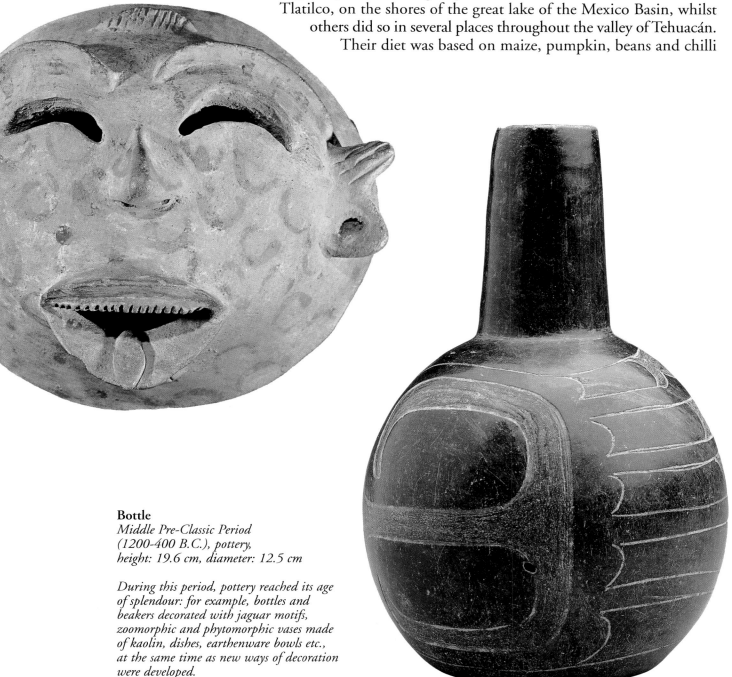

Pectoral Mask
*Middle Pre-Classic Period
(1200-800 B.C.),
pottery, height: 14 cm*

Tlatilco is the most important site of the period of transition towards the first villages in the centre of Mexico. Although its basic characteristics are unfortunately unknown because Mexico City has been built on top of the site, 340 tombs were excavated in which figurines and pottery had been placed as offerings.

Bottle
*Middle Pre-Classic Period
(1200-400 B.C.), pottery,
height: 19.6 cm, diameter: 12.5 cm*

During this period, pottery reached its age of splendour: for example, bottles and beakers decorated with jaguar motifs, zoomorphic and phytomorphic vases made of kaolin, dishes, earthenware bowls etc., at the same time as new ways of decoration were developed.

Vase or Bottle
Middle or Late Pre-Classic Period
(ca. 1200 B.C.- A.D. 1), pottery,
height: 21.7 cm, diameter: 16 cm

*During the Pre-Classic Period, various
methods were employed to decorate pottery.
This bottle found in Tlapacoya, whose
shape was inspired by plants such as
gourds, was stuccoed and then painted, a
technique that would become well-
renowned in later Teotihuacan pottery.*

Female Figure
Middle or Late Pre-Classic Period
(ca. 1200 B.C.- A.D. 1),
terra-cotta or clay

*During the Pre-Classic Period, female
figures of terra-cotta were a very important
cultural practice. Standing or sitting, they
are nearly always naked and wear ear disks
as well as other types of jewellery and very
elaborate headdresses. They are collective
images of cult towards the feminine force
of nature, in which the fertility of the
earth is associated with that of women.*

Bottle or Vase with the Figure of a Contortionist or Acrobat
Middle or Late Pre-Classic Period (ca. 1200 B.C.- A.D. 1), pottery, height: 25 cm; width: 16 cm

The societies of the High Plateau were not, during this period, equalitarian, but hierarchical. The potters of Tlatilco knew how to represent many aspects of their ways of life, portraying figures whose social status or activity were different to those of the rest of the community.

pepper, complemented with game or fish, according to the region. Their main crafts were domestic pottery, painted in white, black and a reddish coffee colour on a surface that was either plain or decorated with finely-cut incisions, and hand-modelled figurines.

Throughout the Middle Pre-Classic Period, a higher concentration of population in some rural villages meant that the latter grew into towns. Consequently, more important towns such as Coapexco and Tlapacoya appeared surrounded by other smaller ones. This development parallelly entailed an internal differentiation, reflected in the variety and size of their buildings. On the other hand, the difference between individuals was manifest in the characteristics of the offerings associated with burials, which is synonymous of the appearance of the elite. In turn, the rise in population led to a necessary increase in agricultural production, whilst the incipient flow of trade of the previous period intensified and led to an increase in the variety of products. The Olmec civilisation is the most representative of this age, since it introduced the organisation of a society governed by medicine men or pastimes such as ballgames, music or dancing.

Reproduction of the Pyramid of the Ceremonial Centre of Cuicuilco
Late Pre-Classic Period
(400 B.C.- A.D. 1), painting

A brief period of splendour in one of the most remote parts of the Valley of Mexico led to the construction of this large circular pyramid covered in stone. The 27 metre high platform could have been the place of cult to the ancient god of fire (Huehueteotl), judging from the clay censers bearing the image of this important deity which were found on the site.

During the Late Pre-Classic Period, while farming was carried out on terraces, there was an increase in crafts and trade, astronomical observations began, and numerals were invented in the way of dots and bars –which would lead to the calendar and hieroglyphic writing-, the Basin of Mexico was becoming quite populated. However, the most distinctive feature of this time was the start of religious architecture, the evolution of which can be observed in the stepped bases for temples in El Cerro del Tepalcate, Cuicuilco and Tlapacoya, culminating years later in Teotihuacán, in time, becoming a hegemonic centre of great power and a markedly multiethnic city.

Teotihuacán, the Holy City

Situated about 50 km north-east of Mexico City, Teotihuacán, "the place where men become gods", was the most extensive political and religious enclave in pre-Columbian America and the capital of the civilisation that bears its name. The Teotihuacan people settled principally in the central valleys of the High Plateau, which is where the most abundant vestiges have been found as well as the most characteristic cultural manifestations. However, the extraordinary influence of Teotihuacán was felt throughout a much greater geographical area.

The Teotihuacan culture, with its various stages of development, prevailed for about ten centuries, disappearing approximately toward the seventh or mid-eighth century A.D. after suffering from pillage and fire carried out by the warring peoples that would later consolidate the Toltec empire.

The meticulous layout of Teotihuacán made it one of the most important points of reference of the age and a model of its kind of holy city. The buildings, arranged in rectangular blocks separated by streets and avenues, were placed along a great dividing line. Within this urban layout, the great temples and palaces occupied by government officials and priests stood in the centre, followed by the sumptuous houses of nobles and privileged classes and, on the outskirts, the houses and workshops of the working class.

One of the most outstanding features of the meticulous functioning of the public services was an extensive and effective drainage system. In spite of the aridness of the area, highly developed agricultural techniques allowed the Teotihuacans to have a flourishing economy for the city, which also included the control of raw materials such as obsidian from the Sierra de Las Navajas. Teotihuacán also produced a large variety of manufactured articles which they traded together with others which were not produced locally, meaning that a certain commercial activity did exist.

Mictlantecuhtli, God of Death or Lord of the Underworld
Early Classic Period
(A.D. 100-200), basalt,
height: 12.5 cm; width: 99 cm

Discovered in the square of the Pyramid of the Sun during the excavations carried out in Teotihuacán between 1962 and 1964, this sculpture represents a common belief of all Mesoamerica by which the Sun, when it set, stopped giving light to the Earth, entered the world of the dead and passed through it in order to get to the east in time for lighting up the Earth again at dawn.

Reproduction of *Tláloc's Paradise*
Detail
Early Classic Period (ca. A.D. 400)
fresco painting

The inner walls of the residential complexes of the middle or upper classes of the ancient city of Teotihuacán were adorned with highly-repetitive, stylised, mythological figures and scenes. The most famous is the one called Tláloc's Paradise *at the Palace of Tepantitla, where those who were killed by water or lightning lived an eternal life of happiness and pleasure.*

Reproduction of the Temple of Quetzalcóatl
Detail
Early Classic Period (ca. A.D. 400), glass fibre, polychromatic life-size scale model

One of the most important buildings of Teotihuacán is the imposing Temple of Quetzalcóatl. Featuring four sides, the entablature of the pyramid is made of rubblework, being adorned with alternating reliefs of feathered serpents and fire serpents, symbolising the basic opposition between verdure and life against hot, arid deserts.

As regards the artistic field, we must highlight the monumental character of their architecture, consisting of magnificent giant sculptures. Nearly all of them correspond with an eminently decorative purpose on the buildings, such as the remarkable sculptures and reliefs adorning the façade of the Temple of Quetzalcóatl, one of the most beautiful constructions of this period.

Likewise, the funerary masks, of great realism, together with a large number of figures and ornaments sculpted in fine stone, are another testimony of the exquisiteness of Teotihuacan craftsmanship. Their pottery is distinguished for its simplicity and elegance, one of the most representative kinds belonging to the age of splendour being the round tripod vessels with a lid; especially beautiful are those made for the elite. Besides these, we could highlight the dishes with a ring-shaped base or vases bearing the image of the god Tláloc. A range of techniques are used in their decoration, such as sgraffito, scraped in relief, painted with plaster, and the paint scraped and incised with a laborious technique similar to that known as *cloisonné*.

Teotihuacán was one of the pre-Columbian cities that most abounded in magnificent wall paintings. The inner walls of its temples were profusely decorated with brightly-coloured highly technical pictures, whilst the outer ones also met that decorative need. Many different subjects are portrayed, ranging from the representation of gods and priests carrying out an infinite number of ceremonial duties to strange mythological animals and various scenes of everyday life.

Seated Figure
Early Classic Period (ca. A.D. 400), clay

The representation of the human figure was something which distinguished the ancient people of Teotihuacán. The faces, whether of terra-cotta figures or those sculpted in stone for funerary masks, look so much like real features that we are inclined to think that they correspond with the physical prototype of those peoples.

**Ceremonial Brazier
Representing Quetzalpapálotl**
*Classic Period (A.D. 1-650),
pottery and mica,
height: 56 cm; width: 38 cm*

*The lower part of this typical
brazier has a very simple biconical
shape and is unadorned,
contrasting with the profusely-
decorated lid, consisting of a
butterfly inside the body of a
quetzal, which is a characteristic of
a deity that is frequently
represented, for example, on the
pilasters of the patio of
Quetzalpapálotl Palace, on the
southern corner of the square
called Plaza de la Luna.*

Chalchiuhtlicue, Goddess of Water
Classic Period (A.D. 1-650),
volcanic stone,
height: 319 cm;
width: 165 cm;
weight 16 t, approx.

Judging by her dress, consisting of a skirt and a quechquémitl (short cape with fringes on the front and back), this figure represents a female deity identified with Chalchiuhtlicue as meander lines symbolising water can be seen around her lap. A symbolic stone was probably inserted in the hole on her chest.

Great Toltec Sites

The disappearance of Teotihuacán brought with it a profound transformation in all fields in the central region of Mesoamerica, including the appearance of other centres which became very important, such as Cholula and Cantona in Puebla, Cacaxtla in Tlaxcala, Teotenango in the valley of Toluca, Xochicalco in Morelos and Tula in Hidalgo. The latter is considered to be its capital city, whilst all of them together make up the Toltec civilised area. Each one developed its own culture, combining Teotihuacan characteristic elements and others from the regions with which they established relations and trade. They are united, however, by their fortification works and their marked militarism during the Epi-Classic (A.D. 650-900) and Early Post-Classic (A.D. 900-1250) periods.

The Toltec period was particularly significant for the archaeological development of Mesoamerica due to two extremely important facts: the introduction of metallurgy for the manufacture of various tools and instruments or ornamental objects; and the appearance of the first truly historic records, chronicles and documents, showing the first genealogies of kings, caciques (chiefs) and cultural heroes, together with their exact chronologies and other kinds of important information for reconstructing history.

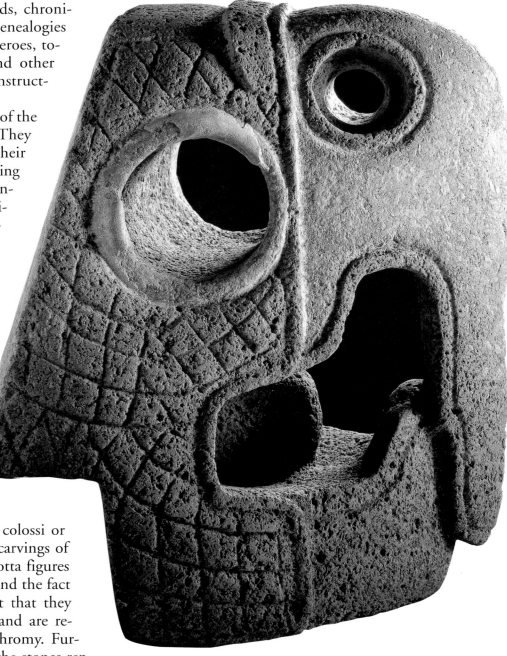

Macaw Head
Epi-Classic Period (A.D. 650-900), basalt, height:56.5 cm; width: 43 cm

This figure of a macaw, a bird associated with the Sun, together with the eagle, the quetzal and the calandra lark, was found placed as an offering at one of the Xochicalo ballgame courts, an activity related to tradition, religion and symbolism. This original stone sculpture is a fine sample of the aesthetical quality of indigenous sculptors.

Their architecture followed the layout of the great ceremonial centres of the age. They adopted Teotihuacan bases for building their first platforms, but adapted them by inverting their proportions. They inherited the concepts of bas-relief decoration, the principle of the serpentine column, descending gods, and other Teotihuacan models. Likewise, being inspired by Maya architectural ornamentation, they introduced small columns, atlantes, pilasters, ballgames and other features especially developed during the Puuc-Chenes period. There is evidence that Tula was in contact with the Maya region since elements that are very similar to those of the Toltec city can be found in the late architectonic style of the holy city of Chichén Itzá, in the Yucatán Peninsula.

The most characteristic Toltec sculpture is personified by the so-called colossi or atlantes, which represent different sized carvings of warriors with their weapons. The terra-cotta figures always appear connected with the gods, and the fact that they were made in a mould meant that they were manufactured in large quantities, and are remarkable for their brightness and polychromy. Further examples of their warlike spirit are the stones rep-

Atlas Representing a Warrior
Post-Classic Period (A.D. 900-1521),
basalt,
height: 460 cm; width: 99 cm

Popularly known as atlantes, four of these columns were found during the excavations at Tula between 1941 and 1943. They consisted of four sections and supported the ceiling of the first chamber of the shrine which was at the top of the Temple of Quetzalcóatl. They represented warriors in full dress and with a bag of copal (resin), a symbol of priesthood and indicating the nexus existing between war and religion.

Vase with the Face of a Coyote-Warrior
Post-Classic Period (A.D. 900-1521),
pottery and mother-of-pearl,
height: 13.5 cm; width: 9 cm

Towards the end of the Post-Classic Period, Tula became the model of Mesoamerican states, which is why not only the Aztecs, but also the last Mayan dynasties, claimed to be descendants of Tula rulers. A symbol of prestige of one of their military orders, the silent howl of the coyote and its mother-of-pearl mosaic fur, envelop the face of a Toltec warrior emerging from the sacred jaws.

resenting skeletons, standard bearers, scrawny figures being devoured by snakes and the tops of buildings in the shape of truncated spirals which symbolise the wind.

The Toltec people also knew how to work wood, bone, shell as well as other materials, and made fine pottery such as the Coyotlatelco type from Tula, formed by simple vases, tripod dishes and bowls painted in red on a yellowish coffee colour.

Another outstanding Toltec enclave belonging to this period is Xochicalco, the "place of the house of flowers", whose military-style architecture in the centre attracts our attention. Some of its most remarkable constructions are the Great Pyramid, the Acropolis, the Pyramid of the Feathered Serpents and the ballgame courts.

The Great Pyramid of Cholula is the largest of all ancient Mexico. Cacaxtla, apart from its fertile lands which made intensive farming possible, allowing a large peasant population to be fed, is known for its excellent mural paintings, where Teotihuacan and Mayan influences joined together to lead to a style of their own.

Wall Painting of Cacaxtla
Classic Period (A.D. 750-850), fresco painting

The pictorial art of Cacaxtla is mainly characterised by the naturalist-design of the human figure. The skill of these artists resulted in impeccable mural painting (using pigments such as Mayan blue, yellows, reds, black and white) and a unique iconography which demonstrated their warlike spirit.

The Long Mexica Pilgrimage

When the Mexicas (more commonly known as the Aztecs, coming from the name of their place of origin, Aztlán, in the north of Mesoamerica) passed through Tula on their migration, the Toltec culture was nearing its end. During their expansive journey, and after a long pilgrimage, the Mexicas reached the Basin of Mexico in the 13th century, on their way finding independent towns such as Azcapotzalco and Culhuacán. They wandered from one place to another until they finally came to an islet of the now extinct lake of Mexico, where the prophecy of their god Huitzilopochtli was fulfilled, which told how they would find an eagle devouring a snake on a cactus, and this was where they founded, in the year 1325, a humble village that in time would become the great Tenochtitlán. During the same period, the Tlatetolcas, a group related to the Mexicas, settled on another islet to the north of Tenochtitlán where they founded Tlatelolco, conquered by the latter in 1473.

The creation of the Triple Alliance with Texcoco and Tlacopan (now Tacuba) in the days of Itzcóatl (1426-1440) and Moctezuma I (1440-1468), saw the beginning of the expansion and confirmation of the power and splendour of the Mexicas, who kept their empire intact until the advent of the Spanish conquistadors in 1519. Thanks to their more sophisticated weapons and to the aid of some indigenous groups subject to the Mexicas, Tenochtitlán withstood three long years of siege, after which it finally fell to the invaders. The capital of Mexico was built on its site, and the Spanish advanced throughout the territory that is now called Mexico. The Spanish left many descriptions of the peoples and their customs.

During the period of Mexica glory, Tenochtitlán reached its age of cultural splendour. It was perfectly laid out, being divided in four quarters which corresponded to the four directions of the universe. The city had many canals and streets, the main ones being built on dikes which, in turn, meant that flooding could be controlled, which extended out into the lake, joining the city to terra firma. There was also a splendid aqueduct which supplied the city with fresh water from Chapultepec.

The Moctezuma Cuauhxicalli
Post-Classic Period (A.D. 900-1521),
basalt;
height: 76 cm; diameter: 224 cm

As a cylindrical sculpture commemorating Moctezuma's rule, the upper part features a hole and a solar emblem with concentric circles of Chalchihuites. The side decoration is divided into three horizontal sections of sculpture in relief: the upper one, being interpreted as a celestial part; the lower one being associated with the monster of the earth; and the central one, with scenes of the conquest.

Simian-Shaped Vase
Post-Classic Period (A.D. 900-1521),
obsidian;
height: 14 cm; diameter: 16.5 cm

Apparently from the region of Texcoco, the famous representation of this ape is another fine sample of Mexica zoomorphic

sculpture. It depicts the action of the god of the wind attracting the clouds heavy with rain and is one of the most valuable objects in the Museum because of the incredible technical skill carried out in its cutting and polishing, bearing in mind that it was made without any kind of metallic tools.

The ceremonial precincts were situated in the centre of the city and, outside, were the palaces and houses belonging to nobles and officials, as well as other community buildings. The tributes received from the places they had conquered provided Tenochtitlán with raw materials, food and manufactured goods, whilst its economy was based on farming, hunting, fishing and gathering. Through trade they acquired exotic luxury articles which were highly esteemed by the noble and governing classes.

Above all, Mexica civilisation stood out for its stone sculptures, through which they expressed a complex range of ideas, beliefs and myths that made up their world and of which the gods were the main theme. Magnificent works have reached us today, one of the most impressive, without any doubt, being that known as the Sun Stone. As regards monolithic sculpture, one of the finest is that of Coatlicue, goddess of the Earth whose religious symbolism materialises the existence of the world and life.

Furthermore, they knew how to give a peculiar style to the manufacture of codices painted on leather or maguey paper, as well as brilliantly developing the art of decorating with ornamental plumes, wood carving and the cutting of hard materials such as obsidian, rock crystal and alabaster. The excellent quality of their craftsmanship can be seen in works such as the headdress of Moctezuma II, and the drums adorned with bas-reliefs, skulls, animal motifs, masks, braziers, feathered snakes, etc.

Huéhuetl or the Eagle and Vulture Drum Called Tlapanhuéhuetl
Post-Classic (A.D. 900-1521), wood,
height: 84 cm; diameter: 50 cm

Music was extremely important to the pre-Hispanic peoples for its meaning, not only in rituals, but also in many everyday activities. Tlapanhuéhuetl is the name given to the vertical drums of the indigenous world, made from a hollowed-out tree trunk, the top being covered with an animal skin.

Reproduction of Moctezuma II's Plumed Headdress.
Detail
Late Post-Classic (ca. 1325-1521),
quetzal feathers, jewels, beads and leather

Aztec crowns were richly adorned with plumes such as this one, considered to be a singular piece of work in its culture. The original is kept at the Ethnological Museum of Vienna, where it has been since 1524, being one of the 158 objects which Moctezuma gave to Hernán Cortés, as an "honorary visitor" when the conquistador arrived in the capital of the empire in 1519.

Oaxaca, Land of the Zapotec and Mixtec

The ancient region of Oaxaca, which approximately comprises the territory of the current state of the same name, was the home of the "Cloud People". It was inhabited by many regional cultures, the most well-known being the Zapotec and Mixtec. The former settled mainly in the Central Valleys and surrounding mountains, although they also inhabited other regions, whilst the latter lived fundamentally in the region of La Mixteca. Monte Albán and Mitla are two of the most interesting sites due to the magnificent state of conservation of their buildings.

The first farming villages of the Oaxaca territory appeared towards 1900 B.C. One of the most outstanding ones, because of its size, is San José Mogote, since it had a continuous growth and a certain social differentiation regarding the dwellings was soon established. Around 500 B.C., it achieved its maximum growth and population, but began being outshone by the glory of Monte Albán, occupied by the Zapotec from 400-300 B.C. until approximately A.D. 900 and which became their capital city. It is curious to observe that the successive stages in which the development of their culture became definite are also called by the same name.

The Zapotec age of splendour occurred between the periods known as Monte Albán III A and III B (A.D. 200-800). They held great knowledge of astronomy, numerals, calendars, hieroglyphic writing, herbal medicine, architecture, jewellery, minor arts, etc. At that time, the ceremonial centre of Monte Albán achieved its maximum expansion, even outshining Teotihuacán, a city which it always rivalled. Examples of the prosperity of the city are the levelling and paving of

Great Jaguar Urn from Monte Albán
Classic Period (ca. A.D. 400-600), pottery, height: 88.5 cm; width: 51 cm

The most-widely produced object in Monte Albán, the Zapotec centre of military, cultural and political power, throughout the period in which it was most in contact with Teotihuacán were funerary urns –symbols of their gods. The threatening feline charm of the jaguar serves here as a polychrome framework for containing the burial fires and receiving the fruit, water and offerings which had to be surrendered to the gods by the deceased.

Pectoral Depicting the God of Sun or Fire
*Late Post-Classic Period
(ca. A.D. 1250-1521), gold,
height: 10.6 cm; width: 7.4 cm*

*Apparently discovered in the city of
Papantla (Gulf Coast), this pectoral is a
splendid example of the sumptuary pieces
elaborated in precious metals by the
Mixtec, whose goldsmithing was
technically complex. Strictly speaking, they
were not objects of personal adornment,
since the motifs represented are deities and
symbols that indicate their ceremonial
associations.*

the *Gran Plaza*, whilst the *Edificio de los Danzantes* ("Building of the Dancers") and the so-called *Edificio J* ("J Building") magnificently represent its architecture.

The Zapotec engaged in farming, hunting, fishing and gathering, making good use of the raw materials available to create weapons, ornaments and other articles, and would also deform their skulls, mutilate their teeth and paint their faces as a way of aesthetic corporal expression.

Their decline was accelerated by the Mixtec penetrations into Zapotec territory between A.D. 800 and 1200. The Mixtec preferred high areas where they could farm, hunt, fish and gather, though, in time, they developed a technology that turned them into remarkable gold, silver and coppersmiths. Their architecture was largely based on the Zapotec style, although they lavishly decorated façades with different kinds of stepped-fret mosaics.

Pot or Vase Depicting Xochipilli-Macuilxóchitl, God of Flowers
*Post-Classic Period (A.D. 900-1521),
pottery,
height: 29 cm; width: 24.5 cm*

Another distinguishing characteristic of the Mixtec was their production of polychrome pottery. This piece modelled in clay and very brightly painted represents the head of Xochipilli-Macuilxóchitl, god of the flowers. A stylised butterfly was also painted around his mouth. The headdress is made up of blue-coloured disks and on his forehead there is a cocox bird, the symbol of this god.

They also produced splendid codices, making this pictorial form a valuable source of information for learning about their genealogies, historic events, conquests, religious concepts, etc. In this way, if the Zapotec excelled more in the intellectual, architectonic and religious fields, the Mixtec did so in the technical skill of their art work.

The gradual political decline of Oaxaca began around A.D. 800-900, which led to conflict between various dominions that were constantly engaged in dispute. However, this did not hinder the development of the cultural exchange and trade within and outside the region. In time, these dominions became tributaries of the Mexica empire once its expansion had been consolidated in Oaxaca in 1458, though the Spanish conquest incorporated both of them at the same time into the domains of New Spain.

Funerary Urn
Classic Period (ca. A.D. 200-800), pottery

The beauty, pride and wealth of the ancient Zapotecs are expressed through their delicate funerary urns which accompanied them to the place of the gods. Their remarkable technical perfection, together with their extraordinarily beautiful decoration, demonstrate the respect they had for their dead, turning them into extremely valuable objects.

Ornamental Disk
Classic Period (ca. A.D. 200-800), pottery and mosaic

The Mixtec used various techniques for their metalwork such as hammering, welding, lost-wax casting and filigreeing, in which they became very skilful. This is how they produced rolled-metal bracelets, disks with embossed motifs, ear disks and pectorals, necklaces or rings that show evidence of their creative imagination.

Pectoral in the Form of a Mask Representing the Bat God
Classic Period (A.D. 1-650), jade, shell and slate;
height: 28 cm; width: 17.2 cm

One of the most remarkable pieces of Monte Albán. This pectoral (chest ornament) depicts a human face wearing a bat mask, a symbol which seemingly originates from Chiapas and Guatemala and is associated with the dark, the Underworld and death. It consists of several plaques of green stone which, apparently, had formerly been set on a wooden frame, today lost.

The Gulf Coast, the Essence of Pre-Hispanic Mexico

The area covering the so-called cultures of the Gulf of Mexico offers a great variety of environmental, ethnical and historical features. It comprises the current states of Veracruz, Tabasco, part of Tamaulipas, San Luis Potosí, Puebla, Hidalgo and Querétaro. It was inhabited by such peoples as the Huastec, Otomi, Nahua, Totonac, Tepehua, Popoloc, Zoque-Mixe and Mixtec, who, in spite of speaking different languages, shared the same cultural background and socio-political and religious development. During the pre-Hispanic period three great civilisations flourished in this region: the Olmec (1500-600 B.C.), that of the centre of Veracruz (600 B.C.- A.D.1300) and the Huastec (600 B.C.- A.D.1521.

The Olmecs chose to settle in the wild area crossed by rivers to the south of the region of Veracruz nearest Tabasco. There, in the far-distant past, they founded the oldest ceremonial centres of Mesoamerica. The best preserved today is that of La Venta. Even though they used clay for their architecture, they constructed spectacular monuments with hard volcanic rock such as basalt. With the help of diorite axes and chisels they carved the great sculptures which characterise their peculiar style, such as the giant heads of San Lorenzo, as well as other symbolic and ceremonial representations, for example the "Wrestler", which probably depicts an athlete in the middle of a ritual ball game.

Other ceremonial objects belonging to the Olmec world which have been found are vases with stylised decoration or small figures which are abnormally obese or showing congenital malformations. The Olmecs were extraordinary traders who were capable of travelling incredible distances in order to obtain valuable stones, especially jade, magnetite, quartz, etc., which they used for making figures, bracelets and necklaces or splendid pectorals (chest ornaments) with images of supernatural feline creatures.

However, the finest testimony of the perfection of Olmec stonework are their ritual masks. Not only were the Olmecs the most advanced pre-Classic culture of Mesoamerica because of their artistic and industrial achievements, but they were also the culture that experienced the widest geographical expansion and greatest supremacy.

The peoples who lived in the centre of Veracruz gave great continuity to the evolutionary process that links the society of villages of the Pre-Classic Period with the ceremonial centres of the Classic one, a period in which many cultures flourished, such as that of the *Remojadas*. It is particularly renowned for its pottery, producing a large variety of highly-expressive, smiling, human figures and vases. El Tajín was the main city of Veracruz during the Classic Period, where complex constructions were built such as great palaces, colonnades, squares, o stepped bases for their temples. A high technical and artistic level in sculpture was also achieved as we can see from the famous *yugos* ("yokes"), *hachas* ("axes") and *palmas* ("palms"), magnificent enigmatic objects

Giant Head
*Pre-Classic Period
(ca. 2250 B.C.-A.D. 200) or
Middle Pre-Classic Period
(ca. 1200-400 B.C.),
basalt, height: 269 cm; width: 183 cm*

The first artists of Mesoamerica were the Olmec sculptors, creators of a characteristic style. Bearing testimony to this is this giant head discovered —out of a total of eight- on the archaeological site of San Lorenzo. Being as they are individualised portraits of rulers, each one is different, the same as the emblem of their helmets.

Hacha Depicting a Human Head
Post-Classic Period (ca. A.D. 600-1300), stone;
height: 28 cm; width: 20 cm

In the centre of Veracruz, during the flourishing of the culture of El Tajín, ritual ballgames rapidly evolved. During this period, extraordinary images of stylised men's heads with ritual symbolic objects were sculpted, like this ceremonial hacha *("axe") in which the person is wearing a fish-like headdress.*

Huastec Adolescent
Post-Classic Period (ca. A.D. 600-1521), stone,
height: 111 cm; width: 39 cm

The stone sculpture of La Huasteca was notable for its high technical quality and the frequent representation of gods or priests. The most famous sculpture is this one of an adolescent, perhaps a symbol of the Young God of Maize. If the figure proves to be rather ethereal for its extreme stylisation, its nudity emphasises its complex engravings.

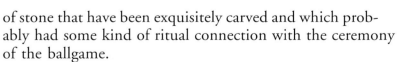

Figurine Representing a Dwarf
Pre-Classic Period
(ca. 2250 B.C.- A.D. 200) or
Middle Pre-Classic Period
(ca. 1200-400 B.C.), jade

*The strange and complex artistic world of
the Olmecs, with their enormous
monuments made of basalt and their
exquisitely-cut jades, also includes the
veneration of deformed beings, considered
to be of a supernatural nature. Their
peculiar sculptural style combines the
simplicity of line with a vigorous
compactness of form, which turns out to be
surprisingly effective.*

Wrestler
Pre-Classic Period
(ca. 2250 B.C.- A.D. 200) or
Middle Pre-Classic Period
(ca. 1200-400 B.C.),
basalt, height: 61 cm; width: 54 cm

*With the exception of the huge portraits of
the rulers, Olmec art was fundamentally a
religious one for its subject matter. This
figure is highlighted amongst the realistic-
style anthropomorphic sculptures, as it is
one of the most vigorous samples of the
primitive art existing in the Gulf Coast.*

of stone that have been exquisitely carved and which probably had some kind of ritual connection with the ceremony
of the ballgame.

As regards the Huastec culture, the sculpture known as "The
Adolescent" of Tamuín (San Luis Potosí) is a fine example of the
sculptural tradition of these people, in which we can identify men
and women associated with fertility cults. The development of this civilisation was so great that it prevailed throughout all the evolutionary
stages of Mesoamerica. What most distinguished the Huastec were
their ornaments made of shell, above all the magnificent pectorals
(chest ornaments) which look like codex pages due to their peculiar
relief. Their architecture, however, is not so technically rich. During
the last period, the Huastec were conquered by the Aztecs, which
led to a hybrid artistic style featuring sculptures of gods and fan-
tastic creatures.

The Supremacy
of the Maya Civilisation

Out of all the pre-Columbian cultures, it is the Mayan civilisation that is regarded as being the most complete and grandest of the New World. Not only do numerous archaeological remains testify their technical, artistic and intellectual advances, but so do the chronicles written by various Spanish monks and historians.

Nearly four and a half million people speak one of the Mayan family languages. The geographical area comprises the states of Campeche, Yucatán, Quintana Roo, part of Tabasco and Chiapas in the south-east of Mexico, a large part of Guatemala and a small part of Belize, El Salvador and Honduras. The region is therefore divided into two large areas: the "Highlands" *(Tierras Altas)*, covering Guatemala and Chiapas, and the "Lowlands" *(Tierras Bajas)*, which, in turn, are divided into two different regions: the north, in the Yucatán Peninsula, with its large natural wells as the only water supply, and the south, where, on the contrary, water abounds thanks to its rivers, lakes and lagoons.

The Mayan culture reached its maximum age of splendour during the Classic Period (A.D. 300-900), as we can see from the construction of numerous important ceremonial centres in the southern part of the territory: Copán, in Honduras; Tikal, Quiriguá and Piedras Negras, in Guatemala; Yaxchilán, Bonampak and Palenque in Chiapas, and Coba, in the south of the Yucatán Peninsula. Towards the end of the Classic Period, in a large area of the latter, new

Urn Depicting Chac, the Indigenous Rain God
Post-Classic Period (ca. A.D. 1300-1400), pottery,
Height: 56 cm; width: 34 cm

Apart from the information provided by the pre-Hispanic codices on the Maya religion, different archaeological objects have demonstrated the relationship between its deities and natural phenomena. The pottery of the late capital of Mayapán is characterised by the magnificent modelling of its figures and the application of paint, of which this figure of the god Chac, holding ritual balls in each hand, is a splendid example.

Reproduction of a Bonampak Mural
Detail
Classic Period (ca. A.D. 200-900) or
Late Classic Period (A.D. 650-900), fresco
painting

Edificio I *of the Acropolis of the*
archaeological site of Bonampak is famous for

its three rooms of mural paintings. They were
painted by order of the heirs of King Chaan
Muan and tell only one story: the ruler's
presentation ceremony, the battle and torture
of the captives, and the celebration of the
victory.

forms of building were developed, which were known as the Puuc, Chenes and Río Bec styles, examples of which are the important remains of Uxmal, Kabah, Labná, Sayil or Chacmultún.

From the 9th and 10th centuries onwards, a certain cultural relationship of the Yucatán with the centre of Mexico led to a stage defined as Maya-Toltec, of which places like Chichén Itzá and Tulum are clear exponents. They all show us how no other pre-Columbian civilisation has bequeathed us with so many and so well-preserved architectonic models.

The same as the last, the exceptional quality of Mayan sculpture - both its reliefs and figures- also surprises us. In all its manifestations (jambs, lintels, memorial stones, steles, etc.) numerous mythological and ceremonial scenes can be seen, accompanied by extensive hieroglyphic texts and chronological inscriptions, sculpted as an account of the life and history of this people. Furthermore, they show us the amazing intellectual progress achieved in astronomy, mathematics and the calculation of time. The Maya adopted a ritual calendar, or *tzolkín*, of 260 days, and a civil one, or *haab*, of 365 days, whilst the combination of both made up the calendaric wheel or cycle of 52 years.

As for lapidary art, the Maya worked preferably with jadeite, carving figurines, pectorals with delicate reliefs and a great variety of other objects. During the Classic Period, Palenque was especially renowned for its beakers and dishes which were either carved in relief or brightly painted, whilst the Post-Classic one (A.D. 900-1521), a period in which a great change occurred in cultural models, saw

Male Head (Palenque)
Classic Period (ca. A.D. 200-900), stucco, height: 43 cm; width: 17 cm

This magnificent sculpture showing us the physical aspect of the Maya, was discovered between the supports of Pacal's sarcophagus.

Chinkultic Disk (Chiapas)
Classic Period (A.D. 591), stone, diameter: 56 cm; thickness: 13 cm

In Mesoamerica, ballgames were not merely an athletic competition: ball courts were a cosmological diagram and balls symbolised the Sun. These disks were placed as circular markers and, in this case, we can observe a bas-relief of a player. A series of hieroglyphic inscriptions surround the scene and enable us to know the exact date.

Chac Mool
*Post-Classic Period (A.D. 900-1521),
stone
height: 160 cm; length: 110 cm*

*The Toltec invaders made the strategic
town of Chichén Itzá their new capital
and the recumbent statues known as* Chac
Mool *their most representative sculptures.
They depict recumbent persons who are
leaning on the floor with their elbows,
their hands on their abdomen, and are
considered to represent a deity or a stone
for sacrifices.*

Pectoral Depicting Halach Uinic
Classic Period (ca. A.D. 200-900), jade

*The Mayan society was divided into three
social castes: nobles, the common people,
and slaves. Within the hierarchy of the
nobles, Halach Uinic was the Great Lord,
a god who held an absolutist, but very
necessary, post. Made of jade, a material
exclusive to the ruling class, this pectoral
shows the profile of one of them whilst he
holds a ceremonial sceptre in his arms.*

the flourishing of the so-called "slatey" pottery, marked by elegant forms, the
beauty of its decoration, and its metallic finish.

The terra-cotta statuettes of the island of Jaina, Campeche, are an extremely
valuable source of information regarding the physical appearance, dress, ceremonies or customs of the daily life of the Maya between the 6th and 9th centuries A.D. In addition to this, the three painted chambers of one of the Bonampak buildings are one of the most important examples of the pictorial
arts of the area. The whole of this artistic heritage allows us to affirm, without any doubt, that the technical perfection and stylistic rigour
of the Maya make them one of
the civilisations which most
contributed to Mesoamerican
art and to the history of
ancient America.

Warrior in Armour in Attacking Pose
Early Classic Period (ca. A.D. 200-650),
pottery, height: 44.4 cm;
width: 23.7 cm

As a sample of the culture of the Tumbas
de Tiro, the interest of this sculpture lies in
the importance the figure of the warrior
had in the unending wars amongst the
seignioralties. Wearing a helmet and
armour, he is clutching a mace, ready to
defend in a dynamic attitude.

The Particularity of the Western Cultures

According to archaeological literature, the complex mosaic of regional and local cultures which, in fact, do not make up a common unity, but have been gathered under the collective denomination of Western cultures, covers the whole of the region going from the River Sinaloa, in the north, to the frontier between Guerrero and Oaxaca. The manifold natural resources of the region greatly influenced the way of life of the peoples who inhabited the vast area comprising the centre and south of Sinaloa, Nayarit, Jalisco, Colima, Michoacán and parts of Guerrero and Guanajuato.

Unlike the cultures developed throughout the rest of Mesoamerica at the beginning of our era, in the West one cannot speak of clearly evolutionary characteristics or elements, as it is even possible that this region became a part of the former only from A.D. 900. Therefore, the archaeology of Jalisco, Colima and Nayarit, for example, is marked by the practical non-existence of splendid works of monumental architecture and stone sculpture such as those found in other regions of Mesoamerica.

Unacquainted with writing and the calendar, they nevertheless knew how to produce a wide variety of interesting, and surprisingly high-quality, pottery. Two of the best-known of these Pre-Classic sites are El Opeño (Michoacán) and Chupícuaro (Guanajuato), the latter being particularly outstanding for its terra-cotta vases and figurines which were funerary objects, as well as for its fine polishing of the ceramic pieces.

Contrary to the rest of the region, the establishment of farming villages in Guerrero is a clear sign of its Mesoamerican past. It is known that between 1400 and 600 B.C. the Olmecs were present in this territory, their influence being evident in the rupestrian paintings in the caves of Oxtotitlán and Juxtlahuaca. Teopantecuanitlán is, without any doubt, the most important Olmec site known today. With the disappearance of the Olmecs, the most significant artistic style to be developed in Guerrero was that known as Mezcala, with a marked Olmec and Teotihuacan influence.

As for the rest of the Western region, we can also mention the different village traditions during the period prior to A.D. 250, maybe the most outstanding being the *Tumbas de Tiro*, found in Nayarit, Jalisco, Colima and Michoacán between 200 B.C. and A.D. 600.

Equally splendid are the examples of a ceremonial-type architecture called *guachimontones*, exclusive to the West and built between A.D. 200 and 700. They are circular constructions that could measure up to 125 metres in diameter, with a central building of several bod-

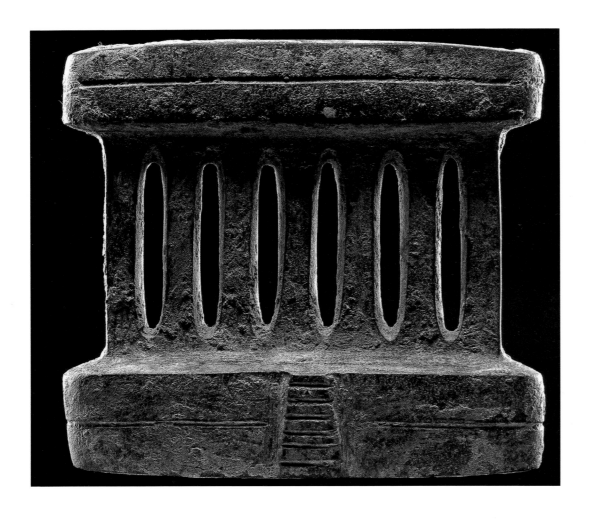

Scale Model of Temple
Classic Period (A.D. 200-900),
green stone,
height: 12.3 cm; width: 9.5 cm

The cultural development of the current state of Guerrero is different from that of the rest of Western Mexico. In the basin of the River Balsas the Mezcala style turns out to be unmistakable, distinguished by its simplified, stylised characteristics both in human figures and masks and scale models, especially of temples, of Olmec and Teotihuacan influence.

Tripod Dish
Post-Classic Period (ca. A.D. 900-1521),
pottery;
height:15.6 cm; diameter: 22.2 cm

The Purépecha introduced new ways and forms of pottery. They added large spherical supports to their vessels, whose shine seems to have been obtained by being polished with wax. Some of the adornment is achieved by the negative technique, protecting the different coloured parts with a resin before baking.

ies. In time, many of the seignioralties that were engaged in successive wars gave rise to village groups dependent on a bigger centre.

Around A.D. 800, the West saw itself favoured by the introduction of gold, silver and copper metallurgy, probably coming from Ecuador, whilst four centuries later, and coming from Peru, they became acquainted with alloy, a technique which allowed them to control the properties of metals and use them for specific purposes.

During the period immediately before the conquest, the Tarasca or Purépecha civilisation consolidated its dominion over a vast territory and managed to develop its own style of art, being one of the few civilisations that was able to defend itself against the Aztec imperialism.

Its main ceremonial centres were Tzintzuntzan and Ihuatzio and, in spite of there not being many examples of their sculpture, which was highly schematic as a result of an almost geometrically-shaped cut, they stood out for their metalwork and their extraordinary way of polishing obsidian.

The Vast Territory of the Northern Cultures

An extensive region of the north of Mexico, including the peninsula of Baja ("Lower") California, did not form part of Mesoamerica, but was shared by another two cultural "superareas", Aridamerica and Oasisamerica, which also comprised part of south-western United States of America. No comparison whatsoever can be made between the archaeological studies of these two areas and those on Mesoamerica, as they have always been considered as peripheral cultures of the latter. They are marked by a limited technological and artistic level, in which various nomad or semi-sedentary groups incorporated only a few characteristics of the richer civilisations that flourished further south. In spite of this, they are an interesting field for anthropological research, their material legacy providing an excellent opportunity for learning about the mechanisms of transculturation between the human groups that inhabited those areas.

With the appearance of the first sedentary and farming groups in what would later be known as Mesoamerica, the area of Aridamerica began its particular differentiation as it continued with its nomad economy. The main way of survival of these peoples

Calendaric Disk
Late Mogollón Period (A.D. 1000-1450), copper, diameter: 25 cm

Found in Paquimé (Chihuahua), thanks to the discovery of the Casas Grandes site, experts have reached the conclusion that this place was a centre for Mexican pochtecas, *a kind of long-distance traders, since the scarcity of metal in Mesoamerica infers that this disk had been made elsewhere.*

Human Skull with Textile Adornments
Desert Cultures, (2500 B.C.- A.D. 1900); human skull, vegetable fibre and shell; height: 23 cm; width: 20.5 cm

The best places for tracing the route of the nomadic tribes of Aridamerica are the shrines and other sites where they buried their dead. Amongst these, we must highlight La Candelaria cave, which is famous for the discovery of mummies lying on one side, bundled up in blankets or matting and accompanied by objects to be used in the Far Beyond.

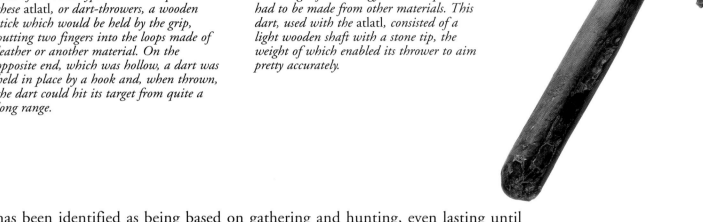

Atlatl or Dart Throwers
Desert Cultures (2500 B.C.- A.D. 1900),
wood and strips of textile,
length: 31.8 cm; width: 8 cm

One of the most typical local weapons were
these atlatl, _or dart-throwers, a wooden_
stick which would be held by the grip,
putting two fingers into the loops made of
leather or another material. On the
opposite end, which was hollow, a dart was
held in place by a hook and, when thrown,
the dart could hit its target from quite a
long range.

Dart and Tip
Desert Cultures (2500 B.C.- A.D. 1900),
wood and stone

Since the peoples of Aridamerica had no
knowledge of metallurgy, their weapons
had to be made from other materials. This
dart, used with the atlatl, _consisted of a_
light wooden shaft with a stone tip, the
weight of which enabled its thrower to aim
pretty accurately.

has been identified as being based on gathering and hunting, even lasting until the age in which the Spanish and nineteenth-century travellers described them in detail.

Aridamerica comprises seven cultural regions: Central and Southern California, the Great Basin, Northwestern Arizona, Southern Texas, Apachería, Northern Mexico, and Baja ("Lower") California and the central coast of Sonora, the last three being situated partially or totally in Mexican territory.

The most important archaeological items come mainly from La Candelaria Cave in Coahuila, and, although they had a funerary purpose, it is believed that they were also employed for everyday use. The human remains, mummified naturally since the arid climate of the region meant that the caves were kept dry, still preserve their hair adornments and many garments, particularly sashes and matting, with strange geometric-style decoration. There are also weapons with stone heads that still have their wooden grip.

Peasant farmers that had gone northwards some centuries before the start of the Christian era gave rise to Oasisamerica, a cultural "superarea" different to the previous one in the farming and sedentary way of life of its peoples. Its expansion began around 500 B.C., reaching its height towards A.D. 1300, when they started to withdraw from the territory, perhaps due to a decrease in rainfall, meaning that crops could only be grown in certain areas, or maybe because of war either between the peoples of Oasisamerica or between themselves and the nomads of Aridamerica.

The region of Oasisamerica basically comprises three areas, Anasazi, Fremont and Hohokam, in the United States of America, whilst those of Mogollón and Pataya are partially situated in Mexico.

Polychrome Pot or Vase
Late Mogollón Period (A.D. 1000-1450),
pottery, height: 16 cm;
diameter: 11.5 cm

The most characteristic crafts representing the age of splendour of the cultures of Oasisamerica were those produced in Paquimé. We are referring to creamy-white pottery painted with red and black curvy and straight lines. Its elegant and varied forms also featured images of animals.

Scale Model of a Section of the Casas Grandes Archaeological Site
Late Mogollón (ca. A.D. 1000-1450)

The research carried out on the Casas Grandes site has allowed archaeologists to estimate that most of the building was started around 1060, declined towards 1261, and ended in 1350. This ensemble of ceremonial buildings, whose structures turned out to be difficult to maintain, were supported by adobe beams, were various floors in height, and were divided up into many rooms.

The main Mogollón site in Mexican territory was Paquimé or Casas Grandes, a place where the cultural exchange with Mesoamerica and other areas of Oasisamerica was extremely important, which can be especially observed in its pottery. Its age of splendour took place between 1100 and 1300, a period in which pyramidal constructions and peculiar courts for ballgames were built.

Ethnography Galleries

If ethnography is taken as being the branch of anthropology that studies human groups from a descriptive and analytic point of view, the part of the building dedicated to it in the museum allows us to acquire an in-depth knowledge of the indigenous cultures of the country. The gallery dedicated to the Introduction to Anthropology on the lower floor prepares the visitor thematically for their visit of the upper floor, where, besides being able to visualise the ways of life of those pre-Hispanic peoples, one can observe the greatness of the richness and diversity of languages that are still alive today throughout the whole Mexican territory. On the arrival of the Spanish, approximately 200 languages were spoken in Mesoamerica, some of which had been split up into 4, 5 or even 12 dialects.

Reproduction of the Inside of a Typical Home of the Gulf of Mexico

This typical dwelling of the Gulf of Mexico area is a fine example of the spirit and contents of the Museum's Ethnography Galleries. Together with other characteristics telling us about their ways of life, the survival of pre-Hispanic elements make the past and present of Mexico an interesting cultural mosaic.

Ethnic Characteristics

In spite of the influence of the different and repeated miscegenations, a trip through the different areas of Mexico helps us to comprehend how Mexicans today still bear many of the ancient pre-Hispanic or Amerindian-type features, especially their straight, black hair, dark skin and eyes. As far as other physical features are concerned, such as height or shape of head and nose, there is a greater difference, which usually make it easy to identify the geographical areas to which Mexican men and women belong, with a rather low rate of error.

Nowadays, neither the languages or the cultures of these peoples are the same as those existing before the Spanish conquest, since, obviously, history has left its mark, but the weight of tradition and legacy can be identified in them.

Interbreeding between the natives and the Spanish gave rise to the Mexican mestizo. Furthermore, they also bore the blood of the slaves brought from Western Africa by the conquistadors during the 16th and 17th centuries.

Later on, the population was administratively and civilly divided into castes according to the individual's degree of miscegenation, which led to different types such as Spanish, *castizo* ("pure-blooded"), Indian, mulatto and negro. After 1810, all divisions of race were abolished and it was stipulated that the natives had to have the exclusive use of their lands. Even so, the sale of these properties facilitated the infiltration of mestizos and whites, circumstance, which together with geographical and cultural factors, led to the current areas of reserve and the pure preservation of the indigenous character.

A great majority of the rural population of southern and central Mexico, as well as small isolated communities of the mountainous and barren regions of the north-west, make up those almost three million natives who live in the country

Purépecha Woman Weaving

The Purépecha gallery shows us the economy of this culture by means of five activities: maize-growing and its relationship with the work cycle and religion; fishing; work in the forests; the manufacture of everyday objects and crafts; and market trade and labour migration as an economic alternative.

Lacquer Ware

The objects produced in Michoacán make this state an extremely interesting place for craft lovers. A great range of crafts are made out of many different materials and produced in various neighbouring communities, such as embroidered clothes, wooden toys, lacquer ware, masks or guitars.

today, who are still proof of the double cultural legacy of their origins and, in quite a few cases, that have hardly been influenced by the modern ways of life of the rest. Their physical characteristics, forms of cult, customs, civil organisation, art or clothing define and distinguish them, and they are proud of their marked ethnocentrism and of their conscious separation from the national culture.

Language and Religion

Nevertheless, there is certainly no doubt that one of the most surprising features is the large amount of indigenous languages that are still spoken today. In accordance with the great number of people that speak them, the main ones are Chinantecan, Huastecan, Mazahua, Mazatecan, Mixe and Zoque, Mixtecan, Náhu-atl, Otomian, Tarahumaran, Tarascan, Totonacan, Tzeltalan and Tzotzil, Yaqui and Mayo, Yucatecan and Zapotecan. They can all be classified in linguistic families, highlighting the following: Uto-Aztecan, Mayan, Mixe, Totonacan, Otopamean, Oaxacan and Chinantecan. Each one includes a number of languages and local variants, which, in some cases, are so diverse that neighbour-

Huichol Woman in the Gran Nayar Gallery

The most distinguishing feature of Huichol clothes is their colour. Women wear cotton shirts and underskirts which are richly-embroidered with coloured thread. Some Huichol families live around their pagan oratory or in larger villages that have a ceremonial centre.

Otopame Wickerwork

The Otopames employ a great variety of techniques and materials for making their crafts, textiles and wickerwork. Especially renowned for their skill in the latter, they create objects of all shapes and sizes, while their characteristics allow us to identify the area of production quite easily.

Sarape, or Poncho, from the Gulf Coast Area

The different designs and colours of ponchos usually have to do with the region where they are made. Unlike in other places, the Mexican poncho, consisting of a woollen or cotton blanket trimmed in bright colours, is worn folded, on one shoulder and is called a sarape.

Dancing Masks and Violin

Amongst the peoples of the Northwest, many elements of the culture of New Spain are kept alive, to different degrees. As for their religion, festivities of brotherhoods, patron saints and the ritual calendar are celebrated with ancient-style dances. They are also accompanied by instruments such as the violin, the guitar and the flute.

ing villages cannot understand one another. This is an example of the cultural diversity still existing in Mexico today.

Another pre-Hispanic feature still surviving in the indigenous world is the political-religious organisation of their communities. Within this mosaic, the figure of the mayor or town councillor can still be found, coming from the political organisation of the Colony, next to which are those of a religious type, such as that of *alférez*, steward, verger and treasurer. Whereas the civil posts can be chosen by election, the religious ones are decided by turn, the people holding these positions eventually being assigned the rank of an elder or a principal. This status allows their incorporation into a highly respected advisory body.

Crafts and Dress

The richness and variety of the forms and styles of their crafts make this the main legacy of the vast Mesoamerican artistic tradition, whilst the Spanish conquest put an end to their great architectural constructions, monumental sculptures, mural paintings, precious lapidary work and codex illustrating. On the other hand, weaving and pottery-making are still carried out, although the new demand for these crafts, due to tourism, has now put these activities into the hands of men. Other types of handicrafts, such as lacquer ware, the manufacture of musical instruments or masks for dances and rituals, flourished throughout the Colony and subsist thanks to export and trade.

As for indigenous clothing, it has gone through so many changes and fashions, resulting in such a variety of costumes that even amongst peoples of the same group it is possible to identify the village they come from. This is only one more example of how the Mexican people take pride in the indigenous, an inseparable and distinctive part of their rich cultural legacy.

Indian Peoples of Mexico

Although it is an unquestionable fact that the ancient civilisations contributed to forming the characteristic aspects of present-day Mexican culture, it is also true to say that their many common features, for example, their religion, social organisation, architecture, economy, etc., expressed in a different way in each region, to a certain extent facilitated that influence.

Metepec Tree of Life

Cerro de los Magueyes is the historic and geographic symbol which gives the municipality of Metepec its name, situated approximately 80 kilometres from Mexico City. During the pre-Hispanic Period, the Matlalzinca and Náhuatl cultures, of the Otopame group, believed it to be a sacred site, where they could worship their deities and bury their dead.

Hunter and Chinelo

Two very important elements of the Tlayacapan culture (state of Morelos) are its bands of music and Chinelo dancing. Chinelo comes from the Náhuatl word meaning "disguised", and this figure is connected with the three days of feasting that take place before Ash Wednesday. Another typical image is that of the hunter.

In this sense, the most important examples of sites are probably the great *plazas* of Mexico, Cholula and Tepeaca, showing us the primitive layout of ancient indigenous cities, whereas, in the field of painting, artists such as José Clemente Orozco, Diego Rivera, David Alfaro Siqueiros or Rufino Tamayo have known how to reflect the mark of those cultures in their works. But the past has enriched the present not only in the field of great artistic expressions, but also in more folkloric forms such as music or dancing.

As a whole, the Indians of today actually have different antecedents, but, in spite of their initial rebellion and intransigence in order to preserve their ways of life and beliefs, the constant presence of European people and customs ap-

Wedding Ceremony

The scenario of the wedding ceremony is extremely important for most communities. The significance of the new life about to be led by the couple is an essential part of living in society, and the advent of a new civil status must be celebrated and honoured accordingly.

pearing as a result of the Spanish conquest has engendered in them the involuntary, but unquestionable, adaptation of cultural, social and political elements, ways of thinking and beliefs which they have, in one way or another, fit in with their mechanisms of life. And so, for example, the Lacandons, who apparently have fully maintained the culture of pre-Hispanic Mayan peasants, do, in fact, wear wristwatches and enjoy listening to the radio. On the other hand, the western world has adopted elements pertaining to these native cultures, especially those regarding food (maize, chilli, turkey, chocolate) and certain linguistic expressions.

Gran Nayar:
Where Tradition Prevails

The states of Nayarit, Jalisco, Zacatecas and Durango, enclaved in Sierra Madre Occidental, turned out to be a bulwark against the persistent Spanish conquistadors. The latter only managed, in the 18th century, to slightly subject the Cora and the Wirivika or Huichol, the main representatives of the state of Nayarit. Together with the aforementioned natives, the Nahuas and Tepehuanes of the south make up the four indigenous groups living in the region.

The task of Jesuits and Franciscans, in spite of everything, had only an apparent success, because the latent feeling of the natives' own beliefs, rites, and sacred sites was much stronger. In 1767, after the expulsion of the Jesuits, the place regained part of its independence, especially in the region of the Huichol, located to the north-west of Jalisco.

With an economy based fundamentally on farming, the Cora and Huichol also share a religion directly related to the agricultural cult. However, their different characters have made the conservation of their traditional isolated existence and the dedication to crafts the modus vivendi of the latter, while the practical and rebellious spirit of the Cora led them to concentrating on stock farming and the production of articles basically for trade.

Amongst the objects typical of Huichol art, are the votive tablets *(nierikas)*, which are symbolic pictures made of yarn. Another distinctive feature are their colourful attire and adornments, the simplicity of the female costume contrasting with that of the male one. For their religious rituals, they make arrows, calabashes decorated with beads, matting and the famous "eyes of God", which are actually figures made of yarn wrapped around sticks that are used to prevent the souls of the dead from passing through. Deer hunting is an essential part of any important ceremony or festivity, since offerings and ceremonial items are smeared with the blood of this animal, as it is considered to be the food of the gods.

The typical dwelling of the region is a hut with a straw roof, around which a small group of smaller ones are built, each of these being the individual oratory of some of their gods. Important ceremonies and meetings

Mural Representing Huichols

The Gran Nayar gallery exhibits essential characteristics of the Cora and Huichol cultures, regarded as the most isolated in Mexico. Their religion, ceremonies, their system of posts and their crafts are all presented to us, highlighting the elaborate male costume and the richness of their cosmovision.

are held in the so-called *casa real*, made of adobe and stone, with a long corridor inside which there is a rough altar with Catholic saints. There is also the *mayordomo*'s ("steward") house, a religious post, and occasionally a small tent.

Elliptic-shaped shrines with straw roofs are also erected to their gods inside the caves where they are believed to inhabit, whereas inside the so-called *casa grande*, surrounded in turn by small oratories, votive offerings for the gods are laid on a rough altar made of mud. In return for these gifts, they are blessed with divine protection.

The Coras Celebrating Easter

In their Easter celebrations, the Cora indigenous communities situated in the mountainous areas of Western Mexico recall the events related to the Death and Resurrection of Christ. For these and other communities in the country, it means a time of liberation from the Evil which endangers cosmic harmony.

It is important to bear in mind that there are about a hundred Huichol divinities and that each one of them has its own "face"; for example, that of *káuyúumáari*, the messenger between the gods and men, is that of the deer. Most of them are related with the agricultural cycle, and both the *casa grande* and the sacred caves are where the 15 great festivities take place every year, as well as where the ritual directed by a chanting shaman is carried out in accordance with the canticles of the Huichol religion.

The pilgrimage and the honour paid to the peyote -a sacred cactus containing an hallucinogen called mescaline and which grows in the desert of Huirikuta, in the state of San Luis Potosí - is another of the most important acts of the Huichol religion, since a complicated and important ceremony is performed with this plant. Every man must take part in this famous ritual at least once in his lifetime.

This ceremony is held every year between the months of October and November and lasts 40 days. After the preparations, carried out the eve before the fixed date, they pray and say goodbye to their wives. Once the men have begun the process, it is forbidden to wash. However, the mere fact of taking part turns them into priests. The overwhelming hallucinations of a trip of 15 or 20 hours after consuming this cactus containing psychotropic properties inspire the *peyoteros*, together with their past and their future, to make *nierikas* of yarn whose coloured strands reflect visions of the world which turns around Tau, god of the Sun. At present, 11 Indian peoples connect with their cosmogony through the consumption of peyote.

Votive Tablet or *Nierika*

The Huichol way of artistic expression reflects their religious feelings, which are portrayed on a great range of traditional ritual objects, on clothing and by building temples and by making musical instruments. One of their most well-known forms of expression are nierika, *or yarn "paintings", made on a wooden board with wax.*

Reproduction of a Gran Nayar Hut

The main type of housing in this region are huts made of mud walls and straw roofs, although it is quite common to find rectangular houses with stone or adobe walls amongst the Coras. The oratory has a gap above the door so that the gods may look in and let their will be felt in some way.

Festivity of the Virgin

The Purépechas maintain their elements of cult, although they have been altered by modern culture. Dances such as Los Moros, Los Negritos *and the famous* Los Viejitos *are performed on religious feasts. The most remarkable ceremonies are that of the changing of the "post" and that of the dead, which is held once a year in November.*

The Singularity of the Purépecha

The Purépecha inhabit the Tarasca Plateau in Michoacán. The region is divided into: the sierra, an abrupt and wet area full of forests, covering most of the region; the area of Pátzcuaro Lake, including Zirahuén and Cuitzeo lagoons; and the narrow valley known as the *Cañada de los Once Pueblos*. The word *Puréecherio* includes the land, family, ancestors, villages, community, tradition and "the custom", i.e., all which is peculiar to the Purépecha people. They know that they have an unwritten social commitment to uphold the norms regarding individuals, families and the community. The "custom" indicates the specific way that tradition is manifest in each village. It is also present in all the stages of a person's life cycle and in the social events of the community.

Their language is not related to any other of Mexico, although distantly-related languages of South America, for instance, allow us to assume that their ancestors were part of some of the most ancient inhabitants of Mexico. The Purépecha are actually identified with a common history which goes back to the days of the Tarascas. The expansion of their territory was cut short in 1530 when they were overcome by Nuño de Guzmán.

Their subsistence is based on farming, especially maize, wheat and potatoes, although there has been an attempt to introduce cotton or linseed. They live in a wooden hut built on large beams with a shingle roof supported by a wooden frame; these dwellings are also known as "barns" probably because of the loft

Mask with Coloured Ribbons

Amongst the Purépechas, it is the woman who connects the productivity of crafts with the external market. Prices and designs are imposed by the buyers, and one may speak of a wide range of objects depending on where they are produced. One of the most remarkable articles made of wood are masks, an essential component of religious celebrations.

where maize is stored. Sometimes the columns at the entrance are carved in a baroque style. Wood is also used for making furniture, vessels, toys and various musical instruments and farm implements. One of the most interesting items made are the masks used in most of the dances, each one being individualised to represent a particular type.

Besides working with wood, each Purépecha are specialised in one or two kinds of crafts, a general characteristic, on the other hand, of pre-Hispanic

Mesoamerica. Michoacán is particularly renowned for the skill of making pictures with coloured feathers, as well as bronze and copper items.

As for their festivities, there are basically three types: patronal; those dedicated to Virgins, accompanied by *Viejitos* and *Cúrpites* dances; and those consecrated to Christs, for example those held in Patamban.

Otopames,
Masters of the Desert

Originally coming from a vast region of the Central High Plateau, the Otopames (Otomis, Mazahuas, Matlatzincas, Ocuiltecas, Pames and Chichimecs Jonaz) have been defined as "masters of the desert" for the way in which they adapted to this inhospitable habitat. The Chichimecs Jonaz and the Pames today inhabit the states of Guanajuato and San Luis Potosí, in an environment similar to that of their ancestors. There are Otomis in equally arid areas of Hidalgo, and in less

Otopame Crafts

The Otopames show great technical and manual skill in the manufacture of their products. The Pames make hats out of long strips of plaited palm. The Otomis of the Mezquital produce bird cages or small decorative figures and toys, as well as weaving baskets and cases. The Mazahuas make rag dolls dressed in typical costumes.

harsh regions of the same state and in those of Querétaro and Mexico. In the south-west of the latter we find Mazhuas, Matlatzincas and Ocuiltecas, whereas the Otomis of Puebla enjoy a better climate.

The Matlatzincas-Ocuiltecas and the Otomis-Mazahuas are an eminently farming group, whereas the Otomis of the Mezquital Valley and the state of Querétaro are gatherers of wild plants, still maintain a good part of their culture of pre-Hispanic origin and continue living on the exploitation of maguey. From this plant they get paper, needles, *ixtle* for weaving blankets and clothing, *pulque*, a fermented drink that was used in religious ceremonies, and is also used for building their huts and obtaining fuel and fibre for weaving cloth and rope.

The Pame-Chichimecs are a marginal group whose economy is based on rudimentary farming, some crafts and small-scale breeding of sheep, goats and pigs. The Otomis-Mazahuas take advantage of the natural resources of the area they inhabit: they grow maize, beans, gourd, wheat and barley, employing metal ploughs pulled by animals; with small nets they catch fish for their own consumption and for selling in the markets. This means that their economy is more prosperous than that of the Otomis of the Mezquital Valley.

Differences in climate and terrain have been the cause of the underdevelopment of several regions of the country. But geographical diversity also explains the variety in economies and crafts. Mezquital Otomis make baskets and show the process of maguey and its end products, whilst Otomis-Mazahuas are also great silversmiths, producing extremely fine objects, as well as making blouses,

Silverwork

The inhabitants of this area complement their economy with the manufacture of various types of crafts. The Otomi-Mazahuas have proved to be great silversmiths. Here we have a sample of the extraordinary quality of the objects produced, whose details and artistic forms reflect the great skill of their makers.

bags, sashes and the typical *quechquémitl*. They live in houses made of mortar with tiled roofs, and a patio in the middle. An oratory is located on one side with a domestic altar, usually decorated with sacred paintings and flowers.

Wickerwork is carried out all over the country. In some regions, all villages do it, whilst in others, only certain places specialise in it. The materials used (twigs, cane, straw, strips of palm), as well as the interlacing techniques and the objects produced, give a hallmark of distinction to the place where they are made. The variety of systems and materials employed is so wide that a general characterisation of the works cannot be made. Amongst the objects produced, we may highlight the following: hats; imaginatively-shaped bird cages; decorative figures; toys; baskets and cases in the form of cigarette cases or rag dolls wearing typical costumes, some of them being made by combining traditional procedures with other more novel ones.

This shows us the personality of a people who are open to any progress that contact with other cultures might bring them, but without abandoning their ancient traditions. In this respect, the Otomis of El Nith have used their skill to make fine wood miniatures inlaid with shell which they probably import from the Gulf of California. In contrast to this, pottery from the Mezquital Valley is rather poor and simple in comparison with the elaborate forms produced in other states.

A Rich Melting Pot of Cultures:
Sierra de Puebla

This area of deep narrow ravines is where the High Plateau and the Coast meet. It covers an area that crosses the Sierra Madre Oriental perpendicularly, from the High Plateau to the Gulf, limited on the north by Ixhuatlán (Veracruz), and on the south from Tulancingo (Hidalgo) to Zacapoaxtla (Puebla). The region is inhabited by people speaking four living languages (Otomi, Tepehua, Totonac and Náhuatl), belonging to three very different linguistic families. Europeans and Africans came to live here in the 16th century, and the union of these ethnic groups led to miscegenation.

The special geographical characteristics of the region have favoured the integration of diverse ethnic groups, besides preserving traditions such as textile art, certain types of pre-Hispanic dances and certain religious ceremonies. On the other hand, the fertility of the land makes it possible to obtain two crops of maize a year, whilst coffee, sugar cane and peanut growing are becoming more important every day. The shortage of game has turned fishing into one of the main activities of the Otomis, having become very specialised, above all, in the collective fishing of river trout in spring.

Mural Representing the Different Ethnic Groups of Sierra de Puebla

Sierra de Puebla, an abrupt region of high mountains and rugged cliffs, has been home to Nahuas, Totonacs, Otomis and Tepehuas, who share similar cultural characteristics, for centuries. Europeans and Africans joined them in the 16th century. In spite of the passage of time, practically none of their customs have waned.

As for crafts, Otomi and Totonac women are famous for their weaving. The most typical garment is the previously-mentioned *quechquémitl*, the great variety of which allows one to know where the wearer comes from. For example, in Cuetzalan and Atla it is made of a very fine embroidered white gauze; in Huehuetla it is embroidered in relief with coloured yarn. This work has a very long tradition in Mesoamerica, and even in the Bonampak murals several women can be seen wearing gauze clothing. The skirt is usually white, although some Nahuas prefer dark-coloured wool. Men's clothes are much simpler, being a white cotton shirt and trousers and a dark serape. Exceptionally, the Otomis of San Pablito wear a shirt embroidered with beads on their wedding day. The creative ability of these peoples can be seen at the *tianguis* or markets, where every Sunday, in the main square and surrounding streets of Cuetzalan, the natives dress up in their Sunday best and turn the action of buying and selling into something more than a just a way of life. Some of the sellers bring their products from the Totonac region. The Otomis are also known for the manufacture of paper made from the bark of the amate tree according to the traditional pre-Hispanic technique.

Nahua Granary

Nature and religious values are a fundamental part of the Nahua cosmovision; furthermore, land is an important element. One lives on it, obtains food from it, and later inherits it in order to guarantee one's line. This is why, throughout one's family history, many rites are performed to give thanks for the benevolence of the land.

The houses of Sierra de Puebla are rectangular with a roof made of straw and leaves, walls of cane, boards or wattle and daub. Next to them is the *temazcal*, the place where ritual steam baths are taken, but which are used mainly for curative purposes. Although it does vary, generally speaking, it is half-dug into the ground, with low walls of stones joined together with mud and a roof made of wood also covered in soil. In San Pablito there are some individual oratories, whereas those of the Tepehua are of a communal character.

Apart from the prayers offered to the spirits of the Temazcal by officiants-quack doctors, there are other kinds of rites, such as those in which people's spirits and the bad spirits afflicting them are cut out in paper made of amate or other plants; the former are easily recognised because they are barefoot, and the latter because they are wearing shoes. Witchcraft, therefore, plays an important role in their religion, possibly being of European or negro origin. In this way, Otomi and Tepehua quack doctors and fortune-tellers lead a great number of ceremonies called "the custom", especially dedicated to the ancient deities connected with the agricultural cycle.

Oaxaca, the Region of the Clouds

The heterogeneity of the languages and cultures of Oaxaca makes it possible to divide it into three large areas: Mixtec, Zapotec and that of the north of Oax-

Women from Oaxaca

The entire state of Oaxaca is a great ethnographical mosaic which surprises us with the wide range of linguistic groups that still survive today. Likewise, it is interesting to point out how each of the different regions maintain their traditional customs, such as costumes or crafts.

aca. The Mixtec region, to the west of the state, goes as far north as Puebla and as far west as Guerrero. The Zapotec region, with the central valleys of Oaxaca and the Sierras of Ixtlán and Juárez, goes as far as Choapan in the north-west, towards the Pacific Ocean in the south, and beyond the isthmus of Tehuantepec in the east. The northern area goes along the summits and hillsides of the abrupt Sierras of Mixe and Huautla. The clouds that almost permanently cover the high summits where Sierra Madre del Sur meets Sierra Madre Oriental are the distinguishing mark of this vast cultural region.

It is interesting to point out that more languages are spoken in this whole area than in any other state of the country, due to the great number of peoples comprising the rich Oaxacan mosaic. Amuzgo, Cuicatec, Chatino, Chinantec, Chocho, Chontal, Huave, Mazateco, Mixe, Mixtec, Nahua, Tlapanec, Triqui, Zapotec, Zoque and the population with Afro-Mestizo features form a plurality that, nevertheless, enjoys a great community solidarity. Political life is based on a system of civic-religious hierarchy or posts, whilst a cosmic order determines the cycles of life on earth and all beings must be subject to them. Man's search has been that of finding the way to integrate these forces and his raison d'être.

The Mixtec region has an economy of subsistence based on maize, sometimes complemented with products suchas beans, wheat, coffee and sugar cane. In the central valleys, the Zapotec grow maize, wheat, figs, fruit trees and vegetables, whilst in the warm dry lands of the isthmus maize is also cultivated along with beans, sesame, fruit and cocoa, their trade being the women's responsibility. They also have livestock and go fishing, using rafts and canoes with oars and poles, and various types of harpoons and nets.

Mazatecs, Cuicatecs and Mixes grow maize for their own consumption and coffee for selling in the market, whereas most of the Chinantecs and some of the Mazatecs living on the banks of the Papaloapan tributaries grow tobacco and get two crops of maize a year.

Practically every village of Oaxaca has a different costume, although the differences are usually small within some regional common features.

On the other hand, the richness of materials, techniques, forms and styles of their pottery are evidence of the important craftsmanship of the Oaxacan culture, as well as producing palms.

The Gulf Coast: La Huasteca and El Totonacapan

Totonacs, Huastecs and Nahuas inhabit the centre and north of the Gulf of Mexico, i.e. in part of the states of San Luis Potosí, Veracruz, Hidalgo and Tamaulipas. The Totonacs occupy the central area, El Totonacapan, although the principal groups are found in the Sierra de Puebla. The Nahuas live in the region of La Huasteca, alongside the Huastecs and small groups of Otomis and Tepehaus. In turn, Tancahuitz, Aquismón, Tanjalás, Ciudad Valles and Tampamolón, San Luis Potosí, are part of the most important Huastec centres. The abundant water resources of the region also encouraged Otomis, Teenek, Tepehuas and mestizos of African and European descent to settle here.

On their arrival in Totonacapan, the Spanish found two large centres of Totonac population, Tajín and Cempoala, whose inhabitants enjoyed a flourishing trade and who grew mainly maize and cotton.

The Nahuas had colonised various places shortly before the conquest, subjecting other peoples as tributaries, whilst the Huastecs had settled in the region before the Christian era.

Female Figure

Oaxacan pottery shows us the richness of materials, techniques, forms and styles existing in Mexico. San Bartolomé Coyotepec is famous for its bells, decorative figures, pots and other objects which are sometimes painted, clearly contrasting with the bay and glazed green pottery of Santa María Atzompa.

Reproduction of the Inside of a Teenek Hut

The Teenek are the only group related to the Mayan linguistic family that lives outside that area. The Teenek of the Potosí Huasteca employ traditional materials which they obtain from their environment. They use sticks for the framework, palm leaves for the roof, and mud, wattel and daub, wood or bamboo for the walls and doors.

Pitcher or Pot from Chilililco

In the state of Guerrero, pottery is made in Huasca and some communities of Huejutla, Alfajayucan, Chapantongo and Ixmiquilpan. Related to the Nahua groups, we have the fine pottery, for example, of Chilililco (Huejutla), its makers being inspired by pre-Hispanic designs and other elements.

The economy of this area is based on growing fruit trees such as avocado, sapota, lemon and orange trees, besides maize, beans, gourd, chilli and yam. The exploitation of sugar cane and the plantations of vanilla were in hands of the Totonac.

Cotton spinning and weaving forms part of the Totonac woman's tasks, as well as helping out with the farming. She uses the *xoxopaxtle*, or waist loom, to make cloth, napkins, tablecloths, sashes or the famous embroidered *quechquémitl*. Men wear shirts and trousers.

The Nahuas also stand out for their manufacture of textiles, as well as for their pottery, the most more important centre being Chililico. As for the Huastec, their main crafts are usually the making of haversack-type bags made of a local species belonging to the genus *Agave*, and colourful women's dresses.

Housing in the region usually has a rectangular ground plan, although it is sometimes square in shape. The walls are made of cane, wooden boards or the combination of both, whilst the roofs are made of palm or tiles. If they can afford it, the Totonacs partition their house inside, and the whole village helps to build a house whenever a couple are going to get married. Around these houses ovens, primitive distilling apparatus and presses for obtaining sugar cane juice are built, as well as *temazcales* or "bathrooms".

With regard to religion in the region, a certain syncretism prevails, with a mixture of indigenous and Christian traditions. The most significant festivities are those of the local patron saints, where various dances are held, such as those known as *Moros y Cristianos*, *Los Santiagueros* or *Los Negritos*. The one known as *Los Voladores*, currently danced by the Totonacs, Nahuas and Otomis in Totonacapan and other parts of the Sierra Norte de Puebla as well as in the south of Huasteca, is one of the dances which most attracted the attention of the conquistadors. Five dancers take part in it, four of which are the *voladores* ("fliers") and a fifth the leader, all being dressed up in brightly-coloured costumes. Suspended by their ankles tied to the rope hanging from the wooden cylinder fixed at the top of a strong, straight and tall pole, these men begin to "fly" slowly down. The leader performs at the top of the frame in the four directions of the universe, to the sound of his flute and drum, thus symbolising the reference to the calendar and the Sun.

From the 16th century onwards, both indigenous and European doctors began to speak of the magnificent properties of medicine based on local herbs. Their importance has been such that many modern medicines derive from them, for example, cortisone, mescaline and psilocybin.

The Maya of the Plateau and Rain Forest

Geographically, the region is situated below 1,000 m above sea level within the vast territory covering the centre of Tabasco, the Yucatán peninsula, the northwest of Chiapas, the north of Guatemala and a part of Belize. It is inhabited by the Hach Winik or Caribs (called "Lacandones"), the Ch'ol, the Chontal of Tabasco and the Mayan Yucatecs. They live alongside mestizos who speak Spanish and Guatemalan emigrants of Mayan origin that inhabit the rain forests of Quintana Roo and Campeche.

As a whole, it is a generally warm territory, of calcareous soils, humid areas full of rivers or dense green rain forests. The alluvial plains of Tabasco, so marshy that in some parts it is necessary to pile soil up into "ridges" and drain excess water from crops, are where the Chol and Chontal live.

Reproduction of a Mayan Hut of the Lowlands

The ethnographers of the Museum have reflected the atmosphere of one of the typical huts of the Yucatán peninsula, with its cane framework and its straw roof. We can also see the techniques employed for preparing agave thread and how they make it, as well as typical women's clothing.

The Mayan ways of subsistence are one of the features that most distinguish the differences existing among the various ethnic groups. In the north of Yucatán, for example, henequen, the symbol of the region, is grown on common land. The calcareous character of the area means that food crops cannot be grown, which is why so many people are employed in industrial work, such as henequen shredding and rope manufacturing, the end products being basically orientated towards the free market economy.

On the other hand, in the south-east, where thicker tropical vegetation covers the beginning of the rain forest of Chiapas and provides them with refuge, the Lacandons grow maize on cleared ground, as well as beans, gourd, tobacco, fruit trees and tropical trees, which are supplemented with hunting.

With regard to their housing, it ranges from oblong and rectangular-shaped huts made of wattle and daub and palm featuring a roof with two slopes, to the modern houses of the more cultured natives.

The female Mayan costume consists of a long *huipil* (tunic) and a three-quarter skirt, which are both white and embroidered, whereas men wear a short-sleeved shirt and trousers, a hat and sandals. Their most characteristic craft is a wide range of wickerwork, especially straw hats, and Mérida is particularly notable for its fine gold and silversmithing.

Maya of the Highlands Hut and Site

Within the Maya group, the economy of the colonial society was sustained on family farming units and large concentrations of lands. Sugar-cane plantations for obtaining sugar grew on mountain tops and sides, in the valley of Grijalva, the region of Soconusco and the Yucatán Peninsula.

The Maya of the Mountains

The Mayan peoples of the mountains are those who live in the regions of Sierra Madre de Chiapas and Sierra de San Cristóbal. Chiapas, regarded as one of the Mexican states with the highest population of Indians, is also one of the most attractive areas of Mayan culture. The Tzeltal, Tzotzil and Tojolabal all speak languages belonging to the Mayan family, and their ways of life are very similar to those of the neighbouring inhabitants of Guatemala.

The brutality of the conquest altered their social structure considerably, becoming exploited by non-Indians, having to pay tributes, being obliged to do services and losing their lands. With the abolition of the amendment (1720), they could go back to their work in the fields in exchange for carrying out jobs for the landowners. Following the toilsome conditions suffered during the 19th century, the 1910 Revolution changed the situation substantially.

Farming is the main source of food for these Maya, using the crops for their own consumption. They breed sheep for wool, chickens for celebrating magical rituals and pigs for great ceremonies. In almost every household, women know how to spin, weave and embroider, and the men make small benches, hooks and other objects of wood. The Tzotzil of San Juan Chamula are renowned for their splendid carpentry, saddlery and manufacture of huge pots; the Tojolabal still weave on vertical looms with pedals.

Trade-wise, the traditional markets of the Altos de Chiapas are very typical, being famous for the diversity of people, languages, costumes and products that can be found in them.

As for religion, the most conservative groups celebrate farming ceremonies such as the *Cha-Chac* to ask for rain.

The Northwest: Mountains, Deserts and Valleys

The north-west of Mexico covers the states of Baja ("Lower") California states and Sonora, the north of Sinaloa and the west of Chihuahua. The coast and the centre of the region are made up of a vast low plain, whilst the abrupt Sierra Madre Occidental stretches to the east.

The area can be divided into three large sub-regions clearly distinguished in terms of climate, soil, water and other resources: that of the desert, inhabited by Cucapás, Quiliguas, Pai-Pai, Cochimis, Seris and Pápagos who lived off hunting, fishing and gathering; the farmers of the mountain, comprising the Tarahumaras, Tubares, Guarijíos and Pimas, and who would sow to the sound of great rain storms, and the farmers of the valleys, made up of Yaquis, Mayoas, Opatas and Jovas who would take advantage of the sudden rise in the river level for sowing. However, as a result of the Spanish conquest and the work of the Jesuits, rebellions took place that would change their ways of life. As to the languages spoken, they all belong to different linguistic families.

The nomadism of the Seris means that they live out in the open, whereas the Tarahumaras escape from the harshness of the winter by sheltering in the caves of the canyons, although they sometimes build stone houses. In this sense, the authorities of the homesteads, formed by a small group of these scattered houses,

Mural of Mayan Ethnic Groups of the Highlands

Maya country —formed, in the Tierras Altas, by mountainous regions full of the erupting volcanoes of the south of Guatemala, El Salvador and a western strip of Honduras- has always been a source of interest and admiration. The diversity of Indian peoples inhabiting the area turns it into a cultural mosaic.

Easter Celebrations

The indigenous beliefs and religious systems of the Northwest were affected by the Catholic religion more in their forms than in their contents. For these cultures, the principal deities that created the Universe are associated with beings of nature under the mutual commitment that men must comply with their ritual duties and their community.

Typical Crafts

The natives of the Northwest have been making baskets for thousands of years. The Seris regard the sápttim, or large basket, as a sacred object. Once a basket has been completed, it receives visitors who bring gifts which will later be shared out at a "farewell party".

are the traditional quack doctors. From outside, one can hear the sound of the rattle and drum being played in the dances and healing ceremonies, whilst in the villages natives dance to the sound of the violin, guitar and flute.

To the south of Chihuahua, near the region of the Tepehuans, houses built of trunks and stones are more common.

Ulama de cadera or *taste* is the typical ballgame played in the north-west of Mexico, the rules of which date back to pre-Hispanic origin.

Nahua Syncretism

The Nahuas, scattered around a large part of Mexico, are the group that has best adapted to modern times although they still maintain their language intact as well as the rituals of their splendid *fiestas* and dances, introduced after the European conquest. Nahua communities can be found in the states of San Luis Potosí, Querétaro, Guanajuato, Hidalgo, the Federal District, Mexico, Michoacán, Puebla, Veracruz and Guerrero. Each one of these areas has developed its own customs, costumes, cultivation of the land and relationship with the world. Although it is true to say that there are some remarkable differences between them, it does not mean that there are no similarities and coincidences.

A million and half people speak Náhuatl today, the language once spoken by the Tenochcas (the inhabitants of Mexico-Tenochtitlán, also known as Aztecs or Mexicas) and, previously by other Mesoamerican groups in the centre of the country, the moun-

Short-sleeved Blouse

Amongst the Nahuas, each subgroup, region or even village, has its own style of dressing. Every detail reflects a tradition, each form represents a way of seeing the world. The rich embroidery around the neck of this blouse reveals the art and skill of the female hands that make these typical garments.

Festivities in general, particularly those of a religious character, are events which strengthen community relationships. Or should we say, these celebrations are cultural manifestations which transform village life and where we can find a mixture of traditions and times.

tains that limit it and part of the adjacent coasts, from Veracruz to Guerrero. Since it was a language spoken over almost all New Spain, it was used as the general language in times of war and so it extended because the Nahuas reached places, in their role of supporting the conquerors, which, until that time, had been unknown to them.

Both the Nahuas' colonial past and their most recent one, including their ways of life, are, in some way, the reflection or the synthesis of what happened with the other indigenous peoples of Mexico. This way, their popular arts, beliefs, ways of subsistence and curative practices, attire, housing and even their ways of social relationship have a different origin. Furthermore, they showed a great capacity of adaptation to the European techniques of metallurgy, working metals with great skill and combining these techniques with those which they already knew, in other words, modernising their traditional ways.

They are skilled artisans: they know how to work clay, palm, wool, cotton, paper, stone, wax, calabash and wood. The use of masks in dances has the magic function of transforming their wearers into the being which it personifies, whilst their music is made with flutes, drums and string instruments like guitars, violins and harps. Paradoxically, this has not prevented them from enjoying listening to recorded music.

Mask of the Devil
*From Tlalcozotitlan (Guerrero)
painted wood, height: 24,5 cm*

Masks still play a vital role today in indigenous and peasant rites. They permit their wearers to change personality and to adopt the psychology and behaviour required in order to play the part assigned to them within the social or ceremonial context of the celebration concerned.

ALPHABETICAL INDEX